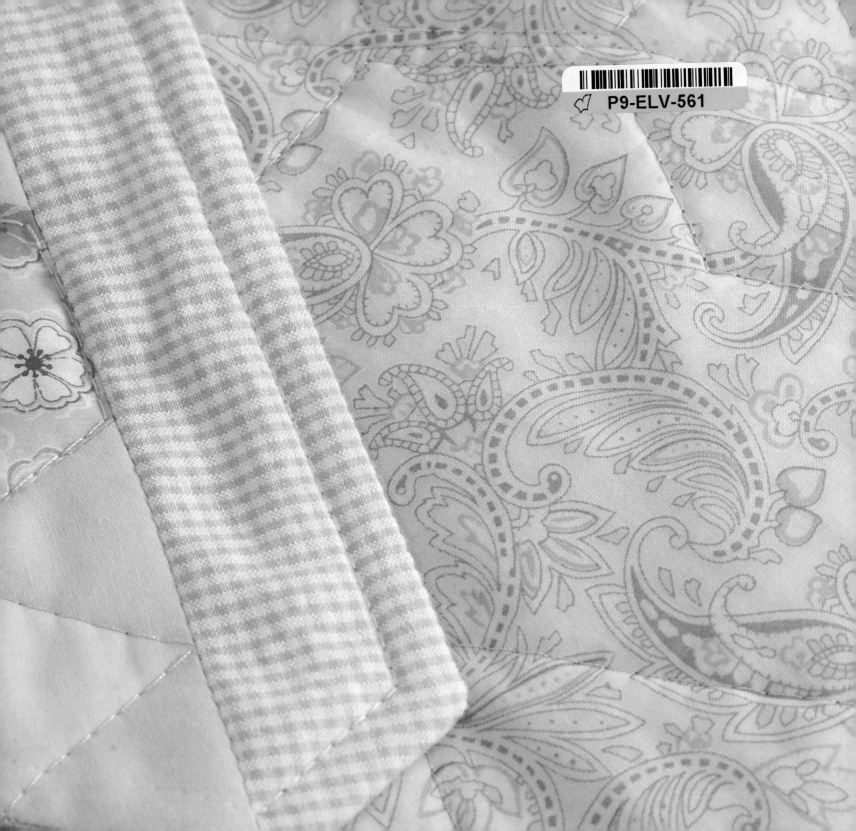

P9-ELV-561

ANNE-PIA GODSKE RASMUSSEN

FLOWER POWER PATCHWORK

PHOTOGRAPHY **CLAUS DALBY**

First published in Great Britain 2011 by Search Press Limited,
Wellwood, North Farm Road, Tunbridge Wells, Kent TN2 3DR

Original Danish edition published as *Flowerpower Patchwork*
by Klematis, 2010

Text and illustration: © Anne-Pia Godske Rasmussen
Photographs © Claus Dalby

Copyright © 2010 Forlaget Klematis A/S
www.klematis.dk
1st edition.

English translation by David Young (translator) and
Ana Madel Morfe (proofreader) at Cicero Translations

All rights reserved. No part of the book, text, photographs or
illustrations may be reproduced or transmitted in any form
or by an means by print, photoprint, microfilm, microfiche,
photocopier, internet or in any way known or as yet unknown,
or stored in a retrieval system, without written permission
obtained beforehand from Search Press.

ISBN 978 1 84448 799 8

Printed in China

**ANNE-PIA GODSKE RASMUSSEN
HAS PREVIOUSLY HAD THE FOLLOWING
BOOKS PUBLISHED:**

Liv i kludene — sy, quilt og appliker, **1998**
Sy tøj til babydukker, **1999**
Mere liv i kludene — sy, quilt og appliker, **2000**
Tøj og tilbehør til babydukker, **2001**
Tag tråden op, **2002**
Træd nålen, **2003**
Noas ark – sy, quilt og appliker, **2004**
Følg tråden – sy, quilt & appliker, **2005**
Sødt og blødt – sy til de mindste, **2007**
Hånd i hanke – sy og quilt, **2008**

PUBLISHED BY SEARCH PRESS IN 2012:

Noah's Ark
Quilt and Sew Country Style

CONTENTS

I have been able to have great fun
experimenting with all the beautiful
fabrics given to me so generously by the
following organisations, so I'd like to say
a huge thank you to:

www.butikenannalunda.se
www.malika-rosa.dk
www.quiltegaarden.blogspot.com
www.speichdesign.dk
www.stofogstil.dk

FOREWORD

Flower power! The term is practically oozing with dynamism and energy. After playing with various designs for some time, and having stitched a fair number of samples in the process, someone suddenly called out the magic words describing the array of samples I'd produced: 'flower power'. After that, everything began to fall into place. I saw the connection between all the samples, and from then on developing the designs presented in this book was a breeze. All the while, a stack of wonderful fabrics in energetic, strong, bright colours and patterns had been piling up. Working with these gorgeous fabrics has been a rewarding and enjoyable challenge.

The result is a series of pretty, floral designs for the sewing table. To store your pins and needles in style, see pages 30–39. For a practical ladies' tool bag with a feminine touch, which can be packed with all the necessary equipment for a group patchwork session, see page 42. Another lovely bag is the knitting bag on page 50 – it is very spacious, with pockets for knitting needles and crochet hooks so they are always at your fingertips. The butterfly quilt on page 86 sprung spontaneously from an idea and was left unfinished for a while, but then suddenly came to life. From there, the hexagon design developed – a fascinating shape that can be turned into many different patterns (see pages 62–79). In particular, it was a eureka moment when I discovered that hexagons can be joined together on a sewing machine!

I also became fascinated by the patterns that can be created from a basic patchwork block, like the half square triangle units on page 11, which can be combined, twisted and turned to create different patterns. Moreover, what seems at first glance to be a rigid form can be softened by the choice of colours, such as in the zigzag patterns on pages 56–59 and the segmented flower centre on page 32.

My greatest wish for *Flower Power Patchwork* is that the book will be used as an inspiration and that it gives you the courage and desire to play, experiment and develop your own compositions in colour and form.

Anne-Pia

EQUIPMENT AND MATERIALS

CUTTING EQUIPMENT

Scissors are essential and a cutting set consisting of cutting board, rotary cutter and ruler makes it easy to cut fabric to specific measurements and with straight edges.

PENCIL AND TAILOR'S CHALK

For drawing on fabric, use a soft pencil or tailor's chalk. Traces left by these disappear with use or in the wash.

MARKING NEEDLE

This is a strong needle that can withstand light pressure. To mark a line along which to sew, score along a ruler or around a template. You can also use this method to mark where to make a fold.

TURNING STICK

A simple flower stick or piece of thin dowel, slightly tapered, is useful for pushing out corners.

NEEDLE AND THREAD

For most tasks with a sewing machine, a needle number 70 or 80 is used. For quilting, you can change to a special quilting needle – ask for advice in your local patchwork shop.

You have a choice between synthetic and cotton thread when stitching on your sewing machine. Fabrics in most colours can be sewn together with mid-grey or beige thread. Visible stitching, such as topstitching, can be worked with a matching colour to give a tranquil look. If you wish to accentuate the stitching, you can sew with a lighter or darker shade of the fabric colour. See also 'Quilting', page 9.

FABRICS

All the designs in this book are made from cotton and linen fabrics, with one design – the rosette pouffe – in upholstery fabric.

FELT

This is used for the needle wallet on page 33. Felt does not fray and can therefore be cut straight into the desired shape.

FIBREFILL

Fibrefill is used as stuffing in, for example, the flower-bud needle holder on page 36 and the rosette pouffe on page 110.

PELLETS

Small plastic pellets, like those used in teddy bears, can be incorporated as added weight. These are used for the pincushion on page 30.

VELCRO TAPES

These comprise two tapes that fasten together firmly and easily. One of the tapes has a soft side; the other tape has barbs that fasten to the soft side.

INTERFACING

This is a thin, stabilising material that comes in various weights and in a fusible or sew-in form. The fusible version can be ironed on to the wrong side of the fabric, making it easy and practical to work with. Vilene is a popular brand.

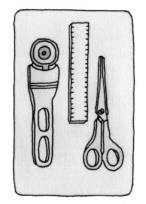
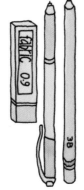

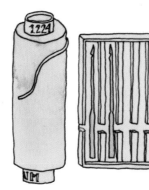

PELMET OR CRAFT INTERFACING

This stabilising material is somewhat stronger than ordinary interfacing. It comes as a fusible or sew-in type. The fusible version is easy to use because it can be ironed on to the wrong side of the fabric. To ensure that the interfacing stays put, it can be tacked in place using the longest stitch length on the sewing machine.

FUSIBLE WEBBING

This is a thin film of glue that is temporarily supported by release paper. It is used to bond one fabric to another and is used in this book for close appliqué (page 88), for example. Popular brand names are Bondaweb and Vliesofix.

VOLUME FLEECE (H630)

Also known as Pellon, this is thin quilt wadding that comes as a fusible or sew-in type. The fusible version can be ironed on to the wrong side of the fabric, making it easy and practical to work with.

TEAR-AWAY STABILISER

This is almost paper thin, but is more flexible than paper. It can be used as a quilt pattern as with the cushions on pages 60 and 82. See also figure 3 on page 9.

INSULATED WADDING

This useful product is used for stiffening the bucket bags on pages 74–79 and as interlining in the oven cloth on page 97.

QUILT WADDING

There are many qualities and thicknesses to choose from. Your choice will depend on personal preference and the project you are working on.

CURTAIN RINGS

Not just for holding up curtains, they make excellent bases for buttons (see page 26 and 74).

SNAP RINGS

These lock like the rings in a ring binder and are used to keep the pages of notebooks together on page 16.

EYELETS

Available in many sizes, they are used to reinforce the holes in the covers of the notebooks (pages 16–19) and the holes in the buttons (pages 26 and 74). For the buttons, choose eyelets with a diameter of 4mm ($\frac{1}{8}$in) and, for notebooks, eyelets of 5mm ($\frac{1}{4}$in). First cut the holes with a pair of hole-punch pliers then fit the eyelets following the manufacturer's instructions. Secure the eyelet tool in a pair of pliers so the parts of the eyelets are squeezed rather than banged together.

TECHNICAL GRID PAPER

This pre-printed paper, available from art suppliers, comes in a number of different designs. The triangular paper is ideal for drawing hexagons – see the templates on pages 118–119.

TEMPLATE PLASTIC

This is simply a sheet of transparent plastic. Patterns can be easily traced on to it and then cut out to make templates. It is available from quilting and patchwork suppliers.

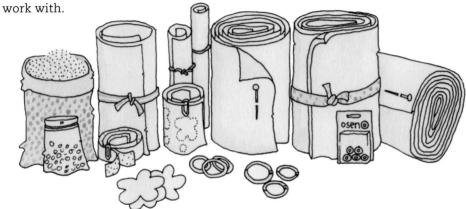

TECHNIQUES

PATTERNS
The patterns and fabric measurements in this book are inclusive of seam allowances, but there are a few occasions when the pattern is used as a template. This is described in the project instructions.

TEMPLATES
If a design is to be used several times, it may be worthwhile transferring it to template plastic. Alternatively, a pattern drawn on paper can be glued to cardboard and cut out with scissors or a rotary cutter.

SEAM ALLOWANCES
The seam allowance for all the projects is the width of a sewing machine's standard pressure foot and is equivalent to 7.5–8mm (a generous ¼in).

JOINING
For joining on a sewing machine, sew with a stitch length of 2.5 or 3.0.

TOPSTITCHING
For the projects in this book, topstitching should be sewn with a stitch length of 3.5 or 4.0 on the sewing machine. This gives an attractive finish.

MARKER STITCHING
For the projects in this book, this is worked, quite simply, with the longest stitch length on the sewing machine, usually 6.0. Use it to provide an accurate marker of a fold or to indicate the position of openings. If the stitching is visible after use, remove it.

APPLIQUÉ
This involves placing a fabric motif on top of a base fabric and stitching it in place (see figure 1). All appliqués in this book are attached using a sewing machine. Appliqué shapes can also be fused in place using Bondaweb/Vliesofix and close stitches (see page 88).

1

2

PIN TUCKS

These are small tucks, which in this book are used to preserve the shape of accordion pockets and emphasise corners (see figure 2). The corners of the ladies' toolbox (page 49) have been stitched in this way, as well as the tea and coffee cosies on pages 94 and 102. The pincushion on page 30 will also have more character if it is sewn with pin tucks.

QUILTING

All the designs in the book are quilted on a sewing machine with a stitch length of 3.5 or 4.0. In some cases, a slightly heavy silk or cotton thread has been used. These will look better than normal thread. Sew a sample and change to a special quilting needle if necessary.

QUILTING WITH TEAR-AWAY STABILISER

Rather than draw on the fabric to be quilted, the motif can be cut out of tear-away stabiliser. This method enables you to use fewer tacking threads.

1 Cut a motif, such as a flower, several times from stabiliser and tack the shapes on to the fabric to be quilted with pins.
2 Quilt around the first motif until you meet the next one, then continue around that one. Repeat until the final motif has been quilted around. Before quilting back again, the centre of a flower can be hand-quilted. The tear-away stabiliser should be removed as the quilting is completed around it (see figure 3).

QUILTING KNOT

This can be used to secure the threads after stitching. Simply pull the top threads through to the back. Tie the top and bottom threads together, and pull the knot as close to the fabric as possible. Thread the thread ends into a needle and insert the needle down where the threads come up, and up again close by (see figure 4).

SLIPSTITCHES

Slipstitches are used to close an opening neatly, usually after an item has been turned right side out (see figure 5).

BINDING

This is used to cover the raw edge(s) of a fabric piece neatly.

1 Fold a strip of fabric in half with wrong sides together and place it right sides together with the raw edge to be covered (see figure 6a).
2 Fold the overhang at the ends around to the other side. Sew with a presser foot's seam allowance (see figure 6b).
3 Fold the strip over the raw edges and sew it in place using slipstitches so that the machine stitching is just hidden (see figure 6c).

3

4

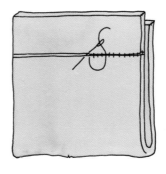

5

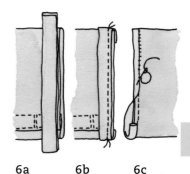

6a   6b   6c

TWISTED CORD

1 Cut off the specified length of thread or yarn and tie the ends together. Fix one end in place around a doorknob. At the other end, insert a pencil or similar (see figure 7a).
2 Hold the strands and twist the pencil, keeping the thread constantly tight. The two strands should be twisted very tightly. Just before they snap, hold around the middle of the twisted strands and fold the end with the pencil over to the other end (see figure 7b).
3 Hold tightly in the middle while the doubled cord is allowed to twist around itself. Tie the ends together.
4 Adjust the length and tie a knot so the string does not unwind.

SELVEDGE EFFECTS

All patchwork fabrics have one of the selvedges imprinted with a colour guide and the names of the designer and manufacturer. Cut off the selvedges to avoid pull in the fabric. If you cut off 5–6cm (2–2¼in) of fabric with the selvedge, these edges can also be used to create decorative effects (see page 21).

1 Start with a strip of fabric without selvedge.
2 Place a new strip on top that has the selvedge still in place so the raw edge of the bottom fabric is hidden, and sew as far out as possible.
3 Lay the next selvedges like roof tiles and sew them as you lay them (see figure 8). Sew in place, preferably with volume fleece underneath because this helps to hold the layers.

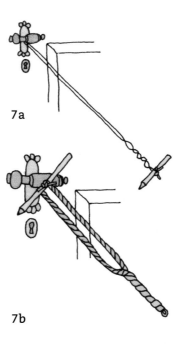

7a

7b

8

FLOWER CENTRES

Some of the designs have an appliquéd flower centre. To form a round flower centre with total accuracy, use the method described here. First cut a circular template – cardboard is extremely well suited to this.

1 Cut a circle of fabric with a diameter two seam allowances larger than the diameter of the template.
2 Cut fusible volume fleece to the size of the template.
3 Centre the volume fleece circle on the wrong side of the fabric circle and iron it in place.
4 Thread a needle with strong thread, knot the end and work running stitch 2–3mm (1/8in) from the edge of the fabric (see figure 9a). Do not finish off the thread at the end.

5 Centre the template on the volume fleece, pull the tacking thread tight and press hard on the front and back of the flower centre (see figure 9b).
6 Slacken the tacking thread and slip the template out.
7 Pull the seam allowance in place and fasten the tacking thread (see figure 9c).

HALF SQUARE TRIANGLE UNITS

Using the technique explained here, you can create a square that is segmented like cake slices, as used for the pincushion on page 32, or the rosette projects on pages 108 and 111. Half square triangle units are also the basic blocks used for the zigzag pattern (see page 56). Cut the initial squares as directed in the materials list for the project you are making.

1 Place two squares of different colours right sides together.
2 Draw a diagonal line on the upper square (see figure 10a).
3 Sew with a presser foot's seam allowance on both sides of the line (see figure 10b).
4 Cut the square along the drawn line and trim off the corners (see figure 10c).
5 Press open the seam allowances – you will have two squares (see figure 10d).

Use the squares according to the project instructions. It is helpful to lay out the squares in the order used for the design – see, for example, the zigzag pattern, figure 11, and the pinwheel arrangement like cake slices, figure 12.

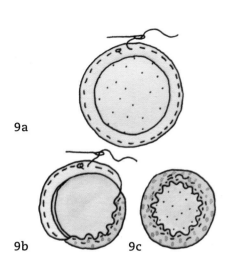

9a

9b   9c

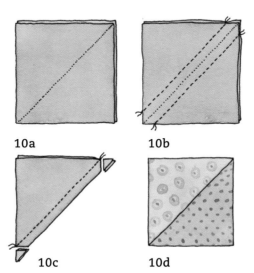

10a   10b

10c   10d

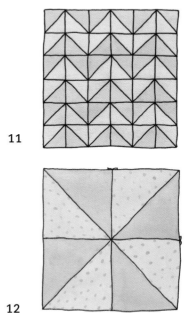

11

12

APRON

This reversible waist-length apron is short and wide with a waist tie. The large pocket on each side is sewn from one piece of fabric. This pocket can be positioned in the middle of the apron or off to one side.

You will begin by making a large piece of patchwork, which can be sewn from multiple pieces of fabric or from just two pieces. The apron measures 48 x 102cm (19 x 40in).

MAKING THE POCKET

1 Neaten one of the long edges of the pocket fabric with zigzag.
2 Fold and press a hem to the wrong side at one of the short ends – first 1cm (³⁄₈in) and then 3cm (1¼in).
3 Unfold the wider hem and then refold it with right sides together. Sew the ends of the hem as shown in figure 1.

4 Turn right side out and topstitch as shown in figure 2.
5 Fold, press and sew the other short end of the pocket in the same way.
6 Press a hem to the wrong side along the side with the zigzagged edge.

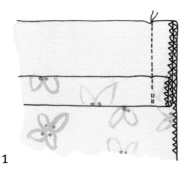

1

2

MATERIALS	
Fabric for the pocket	29 x 68cm (11½ x 26¾in)
Fabric A for the apron	42 x 105cm (16½ x 41¼in)
Fabric B for the apron	57 x 105cm (22½ x 41¼in)
Fabric for the waist tie	7 x 270cm (2¾ x 106¼in)
Fusible interfacing (tie)	3 x 268cm (1¼ x 105½in)

MAKING THE MAIN APRON PIECE

1 Sew the two fabric pieces right sides together along one matching 105cm (41¼in) edge. Press the seam allowances open and sew them in place with topstitching (see figure 3).
2 Divide the piece in two. You can cut one piece 97.5 x 38cm (38½ x 15in) and the other 97.5 x 67cm (38½ x 26¼); with these dimensions the pocket will be positioned in the middle of the apron. Alternatively, cut one piece 97.5 x 27cm (38½ x 10⅝in) and the other 97.5 x 78cm (38½ x 30¾in); in this case, the pocket is positioned on the side of the apron.
3 Turn one of the pieces as shown in figure 4.
4 Position and centre the pocket on the large piece of fabric, so the side with the hem lies towards the inside of the

fabric – in figure 4 the side fastened with pins. Sew the sides of the pocket.
5 Sew the narrow piece of patchwork right sides together with the broad piece and with the long base edge of the pocket (see figure 5).
6 Press the seam allowances towards the narrow piece and topstitch them in place.
7 Fold the patchwork right sides together to the dimensions 48.75 x 103.5cm (19¼ x 40¾in) as shown in figure 6.
8 Sew the short sides, press the seam allowances open and then turn right side out.
9 Topstitch along the sides and bottom edge and then tack up the opening.

ATTACHING THE RIBBON TIE

1 Fold 1cm (⅜in) to the wrong side along the long edges of the fabric strip for the tie.
2 Iron the fusible interfacing in the middle of the wrong side of the strip (see figure 7).
3 Fold the strip in half, wrong sides together, and press it.
4 Open the fold, refold it with right sides facing and sew the short ends together, as shown in figure 8.
5 Turn right side out again.
6 Place the centre of the tie in the middle of the apron at the top (tacked) edge.
7 Unfold one long edge of the tie and position the raw edge of the tie 1.5cm (⅝in) below the raw edge of the apron.
8 Sew the tie in place on the apron, stitching along the fold line of the tie fabric (see figure 9).
9 Fold the tie over the raw edge of the apron so the stitching is just hidden.
10 Sew the ribbon tie from end to end, securing the long edges.

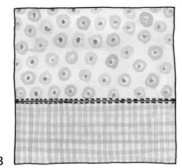
3

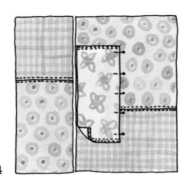
4

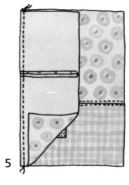
5

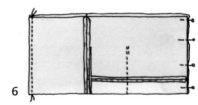
6

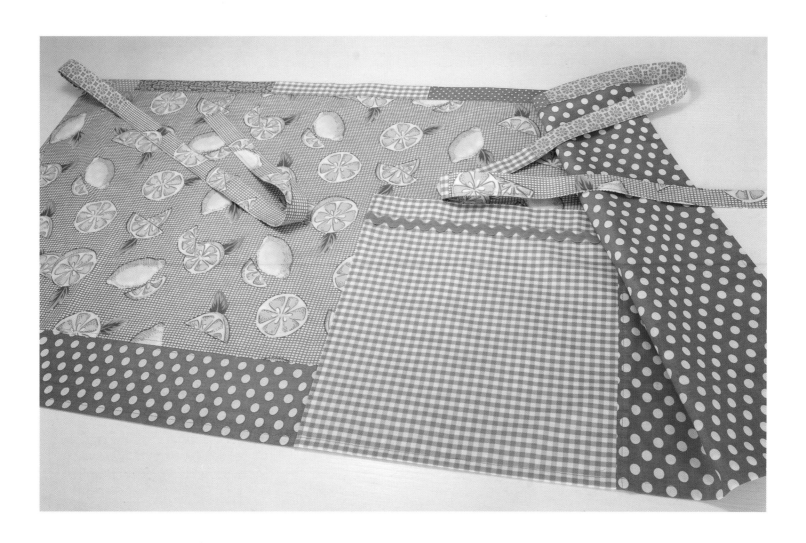

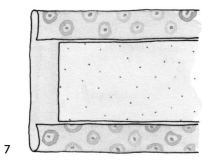

7

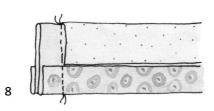

8

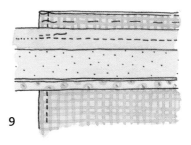

9

NOTEBOOK WITH CLOSED SPINE

These notebooks developed from a desire to reuse envelopes and paper that are blank on the back. The sheets are assembled with snap rings and, to improve the appearance, have a smart fabric cover. The spine of the cover and the snap rings are suitable for a paper stack of 0.75cm (³⁄₈in) for the small notebook or 1.25cm (½in) for the medium-sized or large notebooks.

There are three sizes to choose from: 8 x 8cm (3¼ x 3¼in), 14 x 14cm (5½ x 5½in) and 18 x 18cm (7 x 7in). All three are about 1.25cm (½in) thick. The holes in the cover are reinforced with eyelets. The patterns for cutting the holes in the cover and the paper are provided on page 120.

COVER

1 Position, iron and tack the interfacing in place in the centre of the wrong side of the fabric using the longest stitch length on your sewing machine (see figure 1).

2 Fold a seam allowance to the wrong side at the short ends of the fabric and tack.

3 Fold the fabric as shown in figure 2 and sew just outside the interfacing.

4 Turn right side out, remove any visible tacking and press.

5 Topstitch 2mm (¹⁄₁₆in) from the edge and pull the top threads through to

the back. Fasten them with a quilting knot (see page 9, figure 4).

6 Slide the template-plastic square into the cover and close the opening with slipstitches.

7 Fold the cover and cut two holes, using the widest part of the pattern as your guide (see figure 3 and page 120).

8 Fix eyelets in all the holes (see page 7).

PAPER

1 Cut the paper to the size given in the materials list, making a stack 0.75cm (³⁄₈in) high for the small notebook or 1.25cm (½in) for the medium-sized or large notebook.

MATERIALS

Size	Small	Medium	Large
Fabric	9.5 x 33.5cm (3¾ x 13¼in)	15.5 x 60cm (6¹⁄₈ x 23⁵⁄₈in)	19.5 x 76cm (7¾ x 30in)
Pelmet interfacing	8 x 16cm (3¼ x 6³⁄₈in)	14 x 29.25cm (5½ x 11½in)	18 x 37cm (7 x 14½in)
Template plastic, 2 pieces	7.2 x 7.2cm (2⁷⁄₈ x 2⁷⁄₈in)	13.25 x 13.25cm (5¼ x 5¼in)	17.25 x 17.25cm (6¾ x 6¾in)
4 eyelets, diameter	5mm (¼in)	5mm (¼in)	5mm (¼in)
Paper, about 60 sheets	7 x 7cm (2¾ x 2¾in)	13 x 13cm (5 x 5in)	17 x 17cm (6¾ x 6¾in)
2 snap rings, outer diameter	2cm (¾in)	2.5cm (1in)	2.5cm (1in)

2 Cut two holes in the paper using the narrow part of the pattern as your guide (see figure 4).

3 Put the sheets of paper into the cover and insert the snap rings.

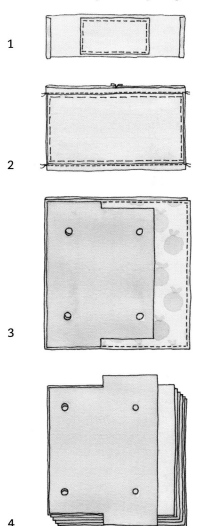

1

2

3

4

17

NOTEBOOK WITH OPEN SPINE

This variation of the previous notebook does not have a spine, making it more flexible with regard to the height of the paper stack.

The three sizes are 9.5 x 9.5cm (3¾ x 3¾in), 14 x 14cm (5½ x 5½in) and 18 x 18cm (7 x 7in) and they are 1.5cm (⅝in) thick. The holes in the cover are reinforced with eyelets. The patterns for cutting the holes in the cover and the paper are provided on page 120.

COVER

1 Position the interfacing on the wrong side of the fabric a seam allowance away from three of the edges, as shown in figure 1.

2 Iron it in place and tack with the longest stitch length on your sewing machine.

3 Fold the fabric right sides together, fold the seam allowances around the interfacing and sew just outside the interfacing (see figure 2).

4 Turn right side out and remove any visible tacking.

5 Press the seams and slide in a square of template plastic.

6 Close the opening with slipstitches.

7 Topstitch 2mm (¹/₁₆in) from the edge without sewing into the plastic.

8 Pull the top threads through to the back and fasten the thread ends with a quilting knot (see page 9, figure 4).

9 Make a second fabric cover in the same way.

10 Place the covers on top of each other and cut two holes, using the widest part of the pattern as your guide (see figure 3 and page 120).

11 Fix eyelets in all the holes (see page 70).

PAPER

1 Cut the paper to the size given in the materials list so that the stack is about 1.25cm (½in) high.

2 Cut two holes in the paper using the narrow part of the pattern as your guide (see figure 4).

3 Put the sheets of paper between the two covers and insert the snap rings.

MATERIALS

Size	Small	Medium	Large
Fabric, 2 pieces	11.25 x 21cm (4½ x 8¼in)	15.5 x 29.5cm (6¹/₈ x 11⁵/₈in)	19.5 x 37.5cm (7⁵/₈ x 14¾in)
Pelmet interfacing, 2 pieces	9.75 x 9.75cm (3⁷/₈ x 3⁷/₈in)	14 x 14cm (5½ x 5½in)	18 x 18cm (7 x 7in)
Template plastic, 2 pieces	9 x 9cm (3½ x 3½in)	13.25 x 13.25cm (5¼ x 5¼in)	17.25 x 17.25cm (6¾ x 6¾in)
4 eyelets, diameter	4mm (³/₁₆in)	4mm (³/₁₆in)	4mm (³/₁₆in)
Paper, 90 sheets	8.5 x 8.5cm (3³/₈ x 3³/₈in)	13 x 13cm (5 x 5in)	17 x 17cm (6¾ x 6¾in)
2 snap rings, outer diameter	2.5cm (1in)	3cm (1¼in)	3cm (1¼in)

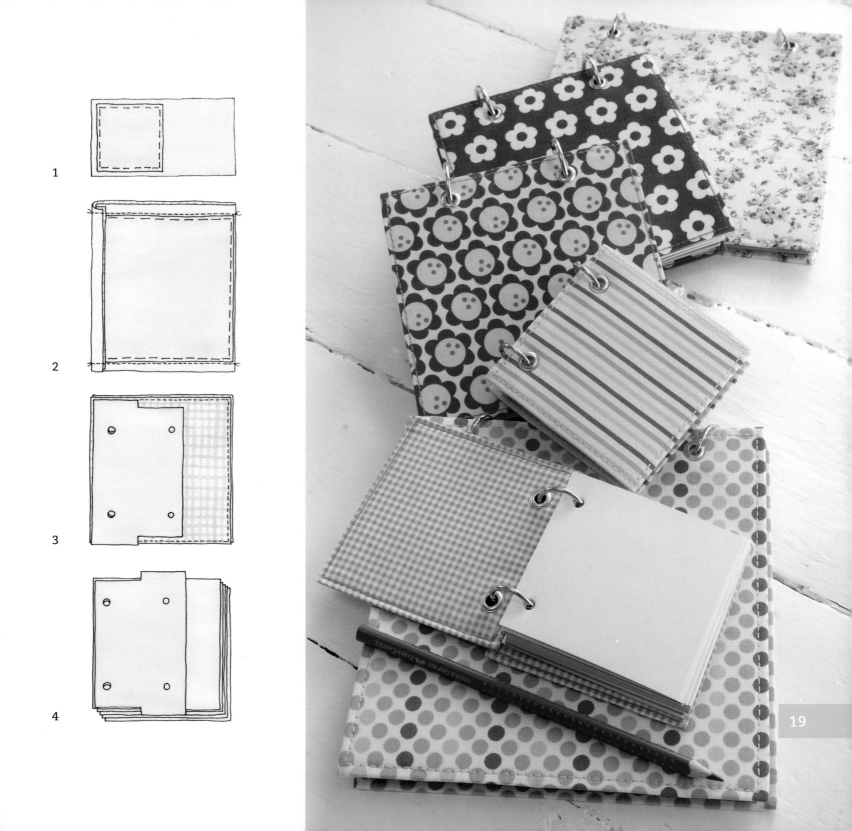

1

2

3

4

PENCIL CASE AND SEWING CASE

Pencil cases can contain many things besides pencils. Here are three different designs, each with its own contents and with pockets and/or elastic holders inside. The first case is tailored for a standard set of 24 coloured pencils, held in place by two parallel elastic strips. The second case has elastic strips to hold sewing accessories and the final case has a combination of accordion pockets and elastic strips.

The pencil case, when folded up, measures 14 x 19cm (5½ x 7½in) and is 3cm (1¼in) thick. The sewing cases measure 14 x 22.5cm (5½ x9in) and are also 3cm (1¼in) thick. The fabric for the outside can be a patchwork, perhaps using the selvedges (see figure 8 on page 10). All the cases have an attractive button and cord closure. The pattern for the case is on page 120. It is a quarter of the pattern (see the instructions below for use).

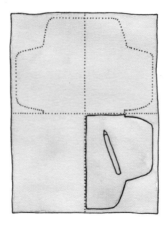

1

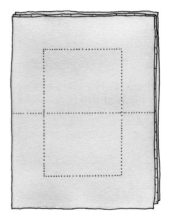

2

MATERIALS

Type	Pencil case	Sewing case
Pelmet interfacing	33 x 43cm (13 x 17in)	37 x 43cm (14½ x 17in)
Fabric for the inside	33 x 43cm (13 x 17in)	37 x 43cm (14½ x 17in)
Fabric for the outside	33 x 43cm (13 x 17in)	37 x 43cm (14½ x 17in)
Volume fleece, 2 pieces	33 x 43cm (13 x 17in)	37 x 43cm (14½ x 17in)
Elastic, 1.25cm (½in) wide	90cm (1yd)	90cm (1yd)
Fabric for pockets		13.5 x 96cm (5¼ x 38in)
1 button		
Yarn for twisted cord	3.5m (140in)	3.5m (140in)

PREPARATION OF INSIDE

1 On the side without glue, draw lines dividing the interfacing in half lengthways and widthways.

2 Draw a quarter of the pattern (see page 120) in each corner as shown in figure 1.

3 Fuse a piece of volume fleece to the wrong side of the fabric chosen for the inside.

4 Fuse the interfacing to the volume fleece.

5 Turn the fabric right side up and mark lines along all the sides 7.5cm (3in) from each edge as shown in figure 2.

6 Mark the centre line, which will be at the bottom of the case when folded (see figure 2).

FITTING OUT

Decide how the case will be fitted out within the resulting rectangle. There are three suggestions on the following pages – for the pencil case, a sewing case with elastic straps and a sewing case with pockets.

PENCIL CASE

1 Measure 5cm (2in) in from each side marking and add parallel placement lines for the elastic strips, as shown in figure 3.

2 Divide and mark 24 equal sections along the placement lines as shown in figure 3.

3 Cut the elastic into two equal lengths.

4 Fold 0.5cm (¼in) to the wrong side at one end of each length of elastic and sew each one in place at the folded end, within the marked rectangle. Sew with a stitch length of 1.5.

5 Make a little arch in the elastics and sew them at their first section marking. Sew back and forth a couple of times for strength. To achieve uniform arches, a flower stick or thin dowel with a diameter of 4mm (⅛in) can be used as a measure (see figure 4).

6 Continue until you have sewn in all the marked sections.

7 Trim the elastic to length, fold 0.5cm (¼in) to the wrong side and sew the ends in place.

8 Pull the thread ends through to the back and tie them together securely.

9 Continue from 'Joining to the Outside' on page 25.

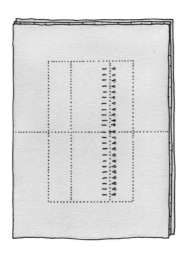

3

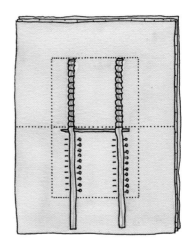

4

SEWING CASE WITH ELASTIC

Equipment of different sizes can be positioned in different directions, but they must not go across the bottom (at the fold). Scissors, a rotary cutter and a ruler can each be fixed with elastic in two places. Smaller items can be secured with elastic around the middle. On each side of the larger items, such as scissors and rotary cutters, allow for 0.5cm (¼in) extra space.

The arches made in the elastic should be sufficiently tight so that the objects they hold stay in place, but not so tight that they bend the case.

1 Plan the location of the equipment within the marked rectangle and mark the placements.

2 Fold 0.5cm (¼in) to the wrong side at one end of the elastic and sew the end in place. Sew back and forth a couple of times with stitch length 1.5.

3 Sew the elastic in place where marked (see figure 5).

4 Trim the elastic at the other end, fold 0.5cm (¼in) to the wrong side and sew in place.

5 Pull the thread ends through to the back and tie them together securely.

6 Continue with 'Joining to the Outside' on page 25.

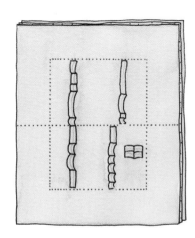

5

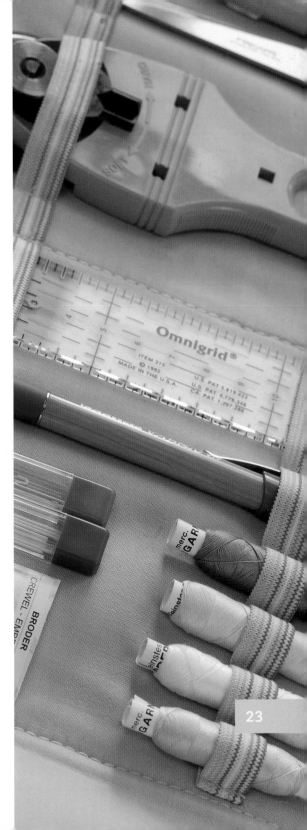

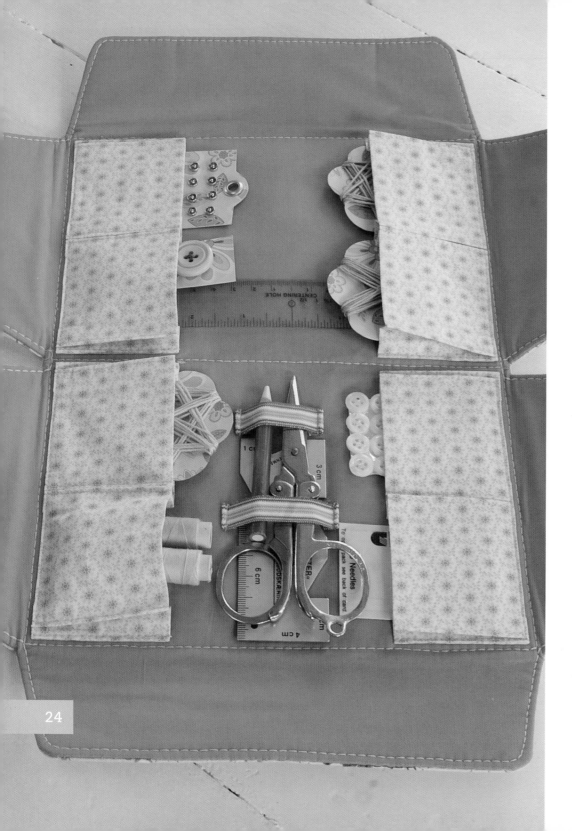

SEWING CASE WITH POCKETS

The fabric quantity listed is enough for four accordion pockets located along the sides of the case. Between the two rows of pockets, there is room for short lengths of elastic as shown in the photograph. Reels of thread or equipment must not be positioned over the fold, which will be at the bottom of the case when closed.

1 Divide the fabric for the pockets into four pieces, each 13.5 x 24cm (5¼ x 9½in).
2 Fold each piece in half lengthways, right sides together and sew the long edges, leaving an opening large

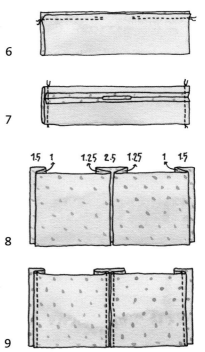

6

7

8   1.5 1   1.25 2.5 1.25   1   1.5

9

24

enough to turn the piece through (see figure 6).

3 Position the seam as shown in figure 7 and press the seam allowances open.

4 Sew the short ends (see figure 7).

5 Turn right side out and slipstitch the opening closed.

6 Fold tucks as shown in figure 8.

7 Sew pin tucks 2mm (¹/₁₆in) from the folds (see figure 9).

8 Position two accordion pockets within the marking on the fabric for the inside of the case.

9 Open the centre pleat and sew in place as shown in figure 10.

10 Secure the sides and lower edge of the pockets by stitching 2mm (¹/₁₆in) from the edge (see figure 10).

11 Pull the thread ends through to the back and tie them together.

12 Place two accordion pockets on the opposite side and sew them in place in the same way.

13 Continue with 'Joining to the Outside', below.

JOINING TO THE OUTSIDE

1 Fuse the volume fleece on to the wrong side of the fabric for the outside.

2 Mark an opening on the inside and outside pieces as directed on the pattern and sew marker stitches.

3 Place the fitted inside right sides together with the outside.

4 Sew along the drawn line, except across the opening (see figure 11).

5 Cut out with a 0.5cm (¼in) seam allowance, except by the opening where it should be 1cm (³/₈in).

6 Cut notches in the seam allowances to all the inward corners.

7 Turn right side out, sew up the opening with slipstitches and press the case.

8 Topstitch across the centre where the fold at the bottom of the case will be and continue, without breaking the thread, around the drawn rectangle, and then all around the outer edges (see figure 12).

MAKING THE BUTTON CLOSURE

1 Close the pencil case by folding the wings inwards. The wing at one end should be folded on the outside to form a flap.

2 Make a button as described on page 26.

3 Mark the location of the button and sew it in place.

4 Twist a cord of yarn (see page 10, figures 7a–7b).

5 Open the cord at the opposite end to the knot and put the loop around the button. Wind the cord around the pencil or sewing case.

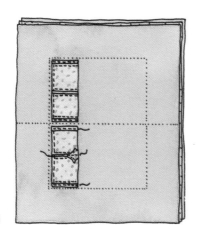

10

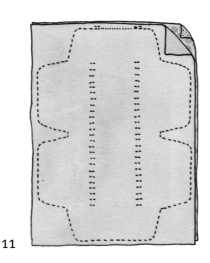

11

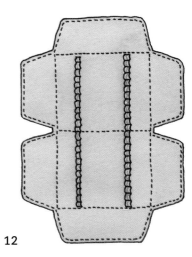

12

25

BUTTON

This handmade button gets its perfectly round shape from the use of a plastic curtain ring as a skeleton. The size is determined by the diameter of the ring. The materials listed are for a ring with a diameter of 4.5cm (1¾in).

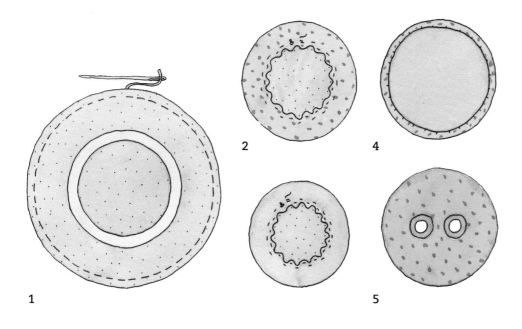

1

2

4

5

MATERIALS

Curtain ring, diameter	4.5cm (1½in)
Fabric to cover the button	8 x 8cm (3¼ x 3¼in)
Fabric for the underside	7 x 7cm (2¾ x 2¾in)
Volume fleece	8 x 8cm (3¼ x 3¼in)
Volume fleece	7 x 7cm (2¾ x 2¾in)
Pelmet interfacing	5 x 5cm (2 x 2in)
2 eyelets, diameter	4mm (¹⁄₈in)
Fibrefill	

1 Iron the 8cm (3¼in) square of volume fleece to the back of the 8cm (3¼in) square of fabric.

2 Draw and cut out a 7.5cm (3in) circle from the bonded fabric.

3 Work running stitch all round, 3mm (¹⁄₈in) from the edge of the fabric, and place the curtain ring in the middle of the circle (see figure 1). Do not knot off the working thread.

4 Pull on the thread so that the fabric tightens around the ring and fasten it securely (see figure 2).

5 Fill the hole in the curtain ring with fibrefill.

6 Draw a 4cm (1½in) circle on the interfacing and cut out.

7 Iron the 7cm (2¾in) square of volume fleece to the back of the matching square of fabric.

8 Draw and cut out a 6.5cm (2½in) circle.

9 Work running stitch 3mm (¹⁄₈in) from the edge of the fabric.

10 Put the interfacing circle in the middle of the wrong side of the fabric circle and then pull on the thread to gather the fabric smoothly over the interfacing. Fasten the thread securely (see figure 3).

11 Place the two fabric circles wrong sides together, centring the smaller one, and sew them together all round with slipstitches (see figure 4).

12 Mark two holes on the button.

13 Cut the holes with a pair of hole-punch pliers and fit the eyelets (see figure 5 and page 7).

KIDS CHECK

michael mi

all rights reserved

modafabrics.com 100%

Made in Japan

Mother's Flower

PINCUSHION

This pretty pincushion is stuffed with fibrefill with a middle layer of plastic-pellet toy filling for added weight. The centre of the flower can be cut from one complete piece of fabric, as in the photograph below, or you can sew a segmented centre (see page 32 for materials and instructions). Patterns for the petals, flower centre and bottom are on page 115.

MATERIALS

Fabric for petals	15 x 30cm (6 x 12in)
Fabric for sides	5.5 x 36.5cm (2¼ x 14³⁄₈in)
Fabric for centre and bottom	12 x 25.5cm (4¾ x 10in)
Volume fleece for petals	15 x 30cm (6 x 12in)
Volume fleece for sides	5.5 x 35cm (2¼ x 13¾in)
Volume fleece for centre and bottom	12 x 24cm (4¾ x 9½in)
Pellet toy filling, if desired	approximately 150g (5oz)
Fibrefill	
2 buttons	

MAKING THE PETALS

1 Iron the volume fleece on to the wrong side of the fabric for the petals.
2 Fold the fabric right sides together and draw the petals and the inner circle, following the pattern.
3 Sew along the curved outer line of the petals.
4 Cut out, adding a 2–3mm (¹⁄₁₆in) seam allowance, and cut notches in the seam allowance between the curves.
5 Cut out the circle in the middle along the drawn line (see figure 1).
6 Turn right side out.

ADDING THE SIDES

1 Centre the volume fleece on the wrong side of the fabric for the sides – there will be a seam allowance of fabric extra at each end. Iron to fuse in place.
2 Mark the seam allowance at both ends and divide the side in between the seam allowances into eight equal sections. Mark these with pins (see figure 2).

1

3 Fold the fabric, wrong sides together, by one of the markers and sew a pin tuck with a 2mm (¹⁄₁₆in) seam allowance (see figure 2).

4 In the same way, fold and sew pin tucks by seven of the marker pins – the final tuck cannot be sewn until the side is sewn together in a circle.

5 Fold the piece right sides together and sew together to form a circle, taking a pressure foot's seam allowance. Press the seam allowances open.

6 Turn right side out and fold wrong sides together so the joining seam is lying right on top of the fold and sew the final pin tuck.

7 Place the petals right sides together with the side and tack together as shown in figure 3.

8 Divide the side into four and mark with pins.

ADDING THE FLOWER CENTRE

1 Cut a piece of fabric 12 x 12cm (4¾ x 4¾in) from the fabric for the flower centre.

2 Cut a piece of volume fleece 12 x 12cm (4¾ x 4¾in) and iron it on to the wrong side of the fabric.

3 Draw a flower centre on top, using the pattern as a guide, and cut out. Alternatively, sew a segmented flower, as described on page 32.

4 Divide the flower centre into four and place it right sides together with the side piece. Put several pins in, so the curve of the circle follows the sides (see figure 4).

5 Sew together along the side, taking a pressure foot's seam allowance.

ADDING THE BOTTOM

1 Divide the remaining fabric and volume fleece into two equal pieces.

2 Iron the volume fleece on the wrong side of each piece of fabric, so it is one seam allowance away from one long edge.

3 Place the pieces right sides together and mark a 4cm (1½in) long opening as shown in figure 5.

4 Sew the seam with a pressure foot's seam allowance next to the volume fleece, except across the opening.

5 Press the seam allowances open.

6 Draw and cut the bottom piece, using the pattern as your guide (see page 115).

7 Divide, position and sew the bottom to the side piece as described for the flower centre, and as shown in figure 4.

FILLING AND ASSEMBLING

1 Turn the pincushion right side out and stuff it very firmly with fibrefill. When the pincushion is barely half full, fill with plastic pellets. Stuff the pincushion firmly with more fibrefill.

2 Slipstitch the opening closed.

3 Thread a long needle with a strong thread, fasten the thread and sew a button in the centre on the top of the pincushion and one on the bottom (see figure 6). Sew up and down and through the buttons two or three times. Pull the thread tight so the buttons sink a bit, and fasten off securely.

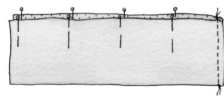

2

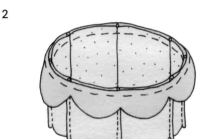

3

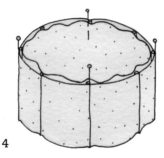

4

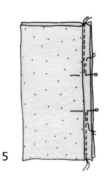

5

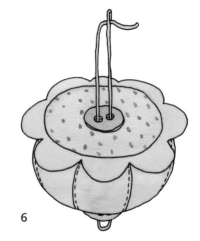

6

SEGMENTED FLOWER CENTRE

The flower centre for the pincushion can be sewn with a two-tone division as explained here.

1 Make half square triangle units as described on page 11, figures 10a–10d.
2 Sew the resulting squares together in pairs and sew the pairs together in the formation shown in figure 7.
3 Iron the volume fleece to the wrong side and draw and cut a flower centre using the pattern as your guide (see figures 7 and 8).

MATERIALS

Fabric in colour A, 2 pieces	8 x 8cm (3¼ x 3¼in)
Fabric in colour B, 2 pieces	8 x 8cm (3¼ x 3¼in)
Volume fleece	12 x 12cm (4¾ x 4¾in)

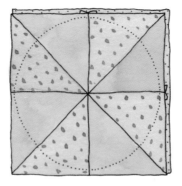

7

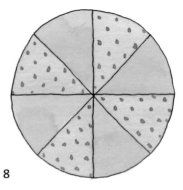

8

NEEDLE WALLET

This handy needle wallet is shaped like a flower with two identical sides. On the inside, felt circles provide a place for storing needles.

It may seem extravagant to bolster a needle wallet with both volume fleece and pelmet interfacing, but the volume fleece preserves the soft surface of the fabric while the interfacing provides a suitable stiffening of the sides. Choose a medium-firm pelmet interfacing.

Patterns for the flower (petals) and the flower centre are on pages 114 and 115.

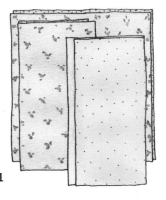

1

PREPARING THE FLOWER FABRIC

1 Cut one piece 15 x 15cm (6 x 6in) and two pieces 8.25 x 15cm (3¼ x 6in) from the fabric for the flower.

2 Cut one piece 15 x 15cm (6 x 6in) and two pieces 7.5 x 15cm (3 x 6in) from the volume fleece for the flower.

3 Iron the volume fleece to the wrong sides of the pieces of fabric. On the narrow pieces of fabric, the volume fleece should be positioned a seam allowance from one end (see figure 1).

4 Put the narrow pieces right sides together and mark a 7cm (2¾in) long opening (see figure 2).

5 Sew together with a pressure foot's seam allowance beside the volume fleece, except along the opening (see figure 2).

6 Press the seam allowances open and put the pieces to one side.

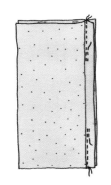

2

MATERIALS

Fabric for the flower	15 x 63cm (6 x 24¾in)
Fabric for flower centres	9.75 x 19.5cm (4 x 7¾in)
Volume fleece for the flower	15 x 60cm (6 x 23¾in)
Volume fleece for flower centres	9 x 18cm (3½ x 7in)
Pelmet interfacing	15 x 30cm (6 x 12in)
Felt	9.5 x 19cm (3¾ x 7½in)
2 buttons	
DMC embroidery thread, or similar	2m (2yd)

MAKING THE FLOWER HEAD

1 Draw two flower centres on the fabric and cut out, adding a seam allowance.

2 Cut two circles of volume fleece to the size of the pattern, centre them and iron them on to the wrong side of the fabric circles.

3 Form two flower centres as described on page 11, figures 9a–9c, and put them to one side.

4 Cut a piece of interfacing 15 x 15cm (6 x 6in) and draw diagonal lines on the side without glue.

5 Centre the pattern for the flower with the help of the diagonal lines. Draw around the pattern (see figure 3).

6 Iron the interfacing to the 15cm (6in) squares of fabric and volume fleece.

7 Mark diagonal lines on the fabric side and a cross on the flower centre with a marking needle.

3

4

5

8 Centre the flower centre with the help of the markings.
9 Appliqué the flower centre in place (see figure 4).
10 Pull the top threads through to the back and tie them together securely.
11 Place the appliquéd fabric side right sides together with the joined square and sew the flower along the drawn line (see figure 5).
12 Cut out the flower with a 3mm (⅛in) seam allowance and cut notches in the seam allowance between the curves.
13 Turn right side out and sew up the opening with slipstitch.

ADDING THE FELT FLOWER CENTRE

1 Draw a circle on the back of the felt using the pattern for the flower centre. Add a 0.5cm (¼in) seam allowance and cut out.
2 Centre the felt circle on the inside of the flower and hold it in place with pins (see figure 6).
3 Sew the felt circle in place from the right side – sew just at the edge of the appliquéd flower centre (see figure 7).
4 Turn the piece over and trim the felt to fit if it unexpectedly sits a little crooked.
5 Topstitch along the curves of the flower, fastening the ends with a quilting knot (see page 9, figure 4).
6 Sew a second flower in the same way.

ASSEMBLING

1 Sew a button to each flower centre without going through the felt.
2 Place the flowers with the inside up, so two petals on each flower meet.
3 Sew the flowers together invisibly where the petals touch (see figure 8).
4 Twist a cord of embroidery thread (see page 10, figures 7a–7b).
5 Open the cord at the opposite end to the knot and put the loop around a button.
6 Close the flower, wind the cord once or twice around the flower and 'lock' it by twisting the cord around the buttons.

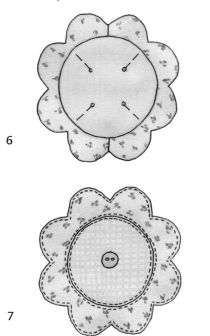

6

7

8

FLOWER-BUD NEEDLE HOLDER

This flower bud has a golf tee for a stalk so that the flower can be planted in a cotton reel. Patterns for the flower bud and sepals are on page 114.

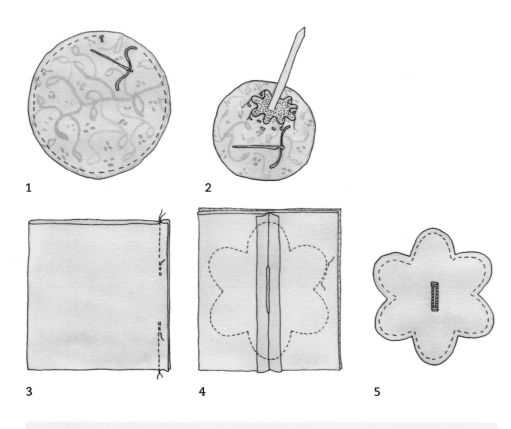

1

2

3

4

5

MATERIALS

Fabric for the flower bud	14 x 14cm (5½ x 5½in)
Fabric for the sepals	10 x 20cm (4 x 8in)
Volume fleece	10 x 10cm (4 x 4in)
Fibrefill	
7cm (2¾in) golf tee	

1 Draw a circle on the fabric using the pattern for the flower bud (see page 114) and cut out along the drawn line.
2 Thread a needle with double thread and tie a knot in the end.
3 Work running stitch 0.5cm (¼in) from the edge of the fabric (see figure 1).
4 Pull the thread up and stuff the fabric firmly with fibrefill.
5 Place the golf tee in the opening and fasten the thread securely (see figure 2).
6 Fold the fabric for the sepals right sides together and sew with a presser foot's seam allowance, leaving an opening in the middle of the stitching of about 3cm (1¼in) as shown in figure 3.
7 Press the seam allowances open with the seam in the middle of the fabric (see figure 4).
8 Draw the sepals on the fabric and place the volume fleece underneath. Sew along the drawn line.
9 Cut out with a 2–3mm (1/8in) seam allowance and cut notches in the seam allowance between the curves.
10 Turn right side out, press and slipstitch the opening closed.
11 Topstitch around the curves.
12 Sew a buttonhole about 1cm (3/8in) long in the middle of the sepals and cut the hole (see figure 5).
13 Thread the golf tee through the buttonhole.
14 Sew the sepals and the flower bud together with slipstitches, so the raw edges on the bottom of the flower are hidden.

TAPE-MEASURE FLOWER

A retractable tape measure is hidden in this flower. The pattern is designed for a tape measure about 5cm (2in) in diameter and about 1cm (³⁄₈in) deep. If the tape measure has different dimensions, the difference can be offset by changing the position of the needle in the sewing machine: a few steps to the right if the tape measure is larger or a few steps to the left if the tape measure is smaller.
The pattern for the small flower centre is used as a template. Patterns for the small and large flower centres, petal and leaf are on page 116.

MATERIALS

Tape measure	
Fabric for the small flower centre	6 x 12cm (2³⁄₈ x 4¾in)
Fabric for the large flower centre	11 x 22cm (4³⁄₈ x 8¾in)
Fabric for the petals	7 x 30cm (2¾ x 12in)
Fabric for the leaf	4 x 15cm (1½ x 6in)
Volume fleece for the small flower centre	5 x 10cm (2 x 4in)
Volume fleece for the large flower centre	11 x 22cm (4³⁄₈ x 8¾in)
Volume fleece for the petals	3.5 x 30cm (1³⁄₈ x 11¾in)
Volume fleece for the leaf	4 x 7cm (1½ x 2¾in)

MAKING THE FLOWER CENTRES

1 Draw two small flower centres on the wrong side of the fabric using the pattern from page 116 and cut out, adding a seam allowance all round.
2 Cut two circles of volume fleece using the pattern, centre them and iron in place on the wrong side of the fabric circles.
3 Make these into two flower centres as described on page 11, figures 9a–9c.
4 Iron volume fleece on to the wrong side of the fabric for the large flower centres.
5 Draw two large flower centres using the pattern and cut both out along the drawn line.
6 Centre the small flower centres on the large flower centres and appliqué them in place (see figure 1).
7 Pull the top threads through to the wrong side and tie them together securely.

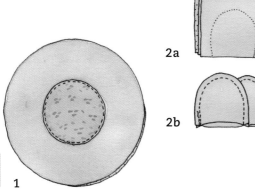

1

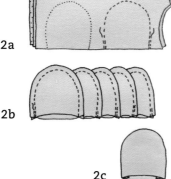

2a

2b

2c

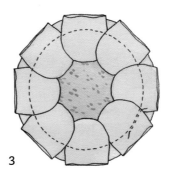

3

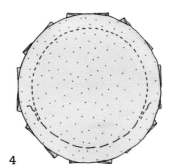

4

ATTACHING THE PETALS

1 Fold the fabric for the petals right sides together to create a piece 3.5 x 30cm (1⅜ x 12in) and draw eight petals with about 0.75cm (⁵⁄₁₆in) between each petal.

2 Iron the volume fleece on to the wrong side of the fabric on the opposite side to the petal drawings.

3 Sew the petals along the drawn line (see figure 2a).

4 Cut out with a 3mm (⅛in) seam allowance and turn right side out (see figures 2b and 2c).

5 Position the petals as shown in figure 3 and sew them in place with a pressure foot's seam allowance.

6 Sew marker stitching as indicated on the pattern on the other flower centre.

7 Put the flower centres right sides together and stitch them together, though over the section with the

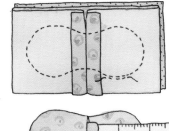

5

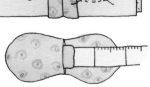

6

marker stitching. Fasten at the beginning and end of the sewing (see figure 4).

8 Trim the seam allowance back on the petals and turn right side out.

FINISHING THE FLOWER

1 Fold the seam allowance to the wrong side by the opening. The stitches and marker stitches should be lying at the top of the fold. Tack the seam allowances.

2 Push the tape measure inside and sew up the opening with slipstitches, leaving a small opening where the tape measure can be pulled out. Remove any visible marker stitches.

MAKING THE LEAF

1 Fold a seam allowance to the wrong side at both ends of the fabric for the leaf and then fold as shown in figure 5. Draw on the leaf using the pattern (page 116).

2 Place volume fleece under the fabric and sew the leaf along the drawn line.

3 Cut out with a 3mm (⅛in) seam allowance.

4 Turn the leaf right side out, slide the end of the tape measure into the opening and sew up with slipstitches (see figure 6).

DELIGHTFUL DIAMONDS

Diamonds are created when cutting using the 60-degree angle on a patchwork ruler. The joined strips should be cut consistently from either the right side or the wrong side of the fabrics.

The materials listed are sufficient for two pieces of diamond-patterned patchwork of 31 x 48cm (12¼ x 19in) or for two pockets for the ladies' tool bag in A3 size (see pages 42–44).

1

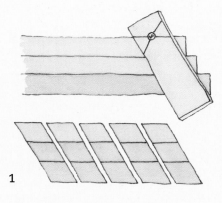

2

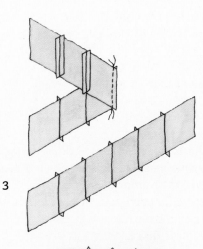

3

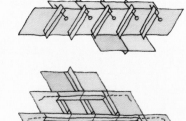

4

5

MATERIALS

Fabrics, 9 different, each	6.5 x 100cm (2½ x 39½in)
Fabrics, 4 different, each	6.5 x 50cm (2½ x 19¾in)

SEWING DIAMOND PATCHWORK

1 Sew the long strips together in threes, taking a presser foot's seam allowance and with the strips staggered by 3cm (1¼in).

2 Press the seam allowances open.

3 Put the ruler on a joined piece, so the 60-degree angle of the ruler is parallel with the side of the strip (see figure 1).

4 Adjust the end of the piece.

5 Cut at least 36 diagonal strips, each 6.5cm (2½in) wide, ideally using a rotary cutter and mat.

6 Cut six diamonds 6.5cm (2½in) wide from each of the short strips.

7 Divide the sections and the individual diamonds into two piles, one pile for each piece or each pocket.

8 Position the sections and the individual diamonds to make up the required piece (see figure 2).

9 Sew together in rows (see figure 3).

10 Sew the rows together, making sure that the diamonds meet at the tips. A seam allowance can be drawn where necessary on the top row, after which the rows can be located together (see figure 4).

11 Press the seam allowances open. The seam allowances at the outer tips lie best if they are pressed outwards. The transverse seam allowances are therefore pressed open (see figure 5).

TOOL BAG POCKET WITH DIAMONDS

See measurements on page 42.

1 Cut the completed patchwork piece to size, using the pocket lining as a guide (see figure 6).

2 Sew the outer pockets for the tool bag as described on page 44 and as shown in figure 1.

6

LADIES' TOOL BAG

This tool bag comes in two sizes. The smaller bag can hold an A4-size cutting board and a 30cm (12in) ruler. The larger one can hold an A3 cutting board and a 45cm (18in) ruler. The A4 bag is 23cm (9in) tall, 34cm (13½in) wide and 7cm (2¾in) deep. The A3 bag is 32.5cm (12¾in) tall, 49.5cm (19½in) wide and 9cm (3½in) deep. Both sizes have thirteen pocket compartments. The outer pockets are divided by the handle, so there are three compartments in each pocket, a total of six compartments. Accordion pockets inside the bag, with two and three compartments respectively, create seven more compartments. A marking needle is a good aid when the folds for the pleats are to be marked (see page 6). As a variation, the outside pockets of the tool bag can be sewn from diamond patchwork (see pages 40–41).

MATERIALS

SIZE	A4	A3
Outer pockets		
Fabric (diamond patchwork) 2 pieces	23 x 33.5cm (9 x 13¼in)	31 x 48.5cm (12¼ x 19in)
Lining, 2 pieces	23 x 33.5cm (9 x 13¼in)	31 x 48.5cm (12¼ x 19in)
Volume fleece, 2 pieces	23 x 33.5cm (9 x 13¼in)	31 x 48.5cm (12¼ x 19in)
Inner pockets		
Fabric, 2 pieces	44.5 x 33.5cm (17½ x 13¼in)	60.5 x 48.5cm (24 x 19in)
Volume fleece, 2 pieces	22.25 x 33.5cm (8 ¾ x 13¼in)	30.25 x 48.5cm (12 x 19in)
Accordion pockets		
Fabric for pocket with 2 compartments	31.5 x 44.5cm (12½ x 17½in)	43.5 x 59.5cm (17 x 23½in)
Fabric for pocket with 3 compartments	31.5 x 50.5cm (12½ x 19¾in)	43.5 x 65.5cm (17 x 25¾in)
Interfacing for 2-compartment pocket	15 x 44.5cm (6 x 17½in)	21 x 59.5cm (8¼ x 23½in)
Interfacing for 3-compartment pocket	15 x 50.5cm (6 x 19¾in)	21 x 65.5cm (8¼ x 25¾in)
Main sections		
Fabric for the main body	45 x 110cm (17¾ x 43¼in)	62 x 150cm (24½ x 59in)
Fabric for the handle	12 x 160cm (4¾ x 63in)	14 x 230cm (5½ x 90½in)
Volume fleece for the body	45 x 110cm (17¾ x 43¼in)	62 x 150cm (24½ x 59in)
Volume fleece for the handle	6 x 158.5cm (2⅜ x 62½in)	7 x 228.5cm (2¾ x 90in)
Fabric for binding	6.5 x 54cm (2½ x 21¼in)	6.5 x 70cm (2½ x 27½in)

MAKING THE OUTER POCKETS

The outer pockets can be sewn from patchwork pieces that are made to the dimensions specified in the materials list. Information on creating diamond patchwork is given on pages 40–41.

1 Place one outer-pocket fabric and lining right sides together and place the volume fleece underneath.
2 Sew together all round, taking a presser foot's seam allowance and leaving an opening of about 6cm (2⅜in) to turn the fabrics out (see figure 1).
3 Cut off the seam allowance diagonally at the corners and turn right side out.

4 Slipstitch the opening closed and press the pocket.
5 Topstitch along the top edge of the pocket.
6 Make a second pocket in the same way.
7 Set the pockets aside for later assembly.

MAKING THE INNER POCKETS

1 Fold one inner-pocket fabric right sides together. For the A4 size, the dimensions should be 22.25 x 33.5cm (8¾ x 13¼in). For the A3 size, the dimensions should be 30.25 x 48.5cm (12 x 19in).

2 Place the volume fleece underneath and sew along the three raw edges, leaving an opening of about 6cm (2⅜in) as shown in figure 2.
3 Trim off the seam allowance diagonally at the corners and turn right side out.
4 Slipstitch the opening closed and press the pocket.
5 Topstitch along the top edge of the pocket.
6 Make a second pocket in the same way.
7 Set the pockets aside for later assembly with the accordion pockets.

MAKING THE ACCORDION POCKETS

1 Fold one accordion-pocket fabric right sides together. For the A4 size, the dimensions should be 15.75 x

1

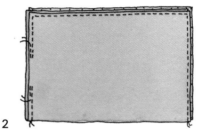

2

44.5cm (6¼ x 17½in) for a pocket with two compartments and 15.75 x 50.5cm (6¼ x 19¾in) for one with three. For A3 size, the dimensions should be 21.75 x 59.5cm (8½ x 23½in) and 21.75 x 65.5cm (8½ x 25¾in) respectively.

2 Sew with a presser foot's seam allowance and leaving an opening (see figure 3).

3 Press the seam allowances open with the seam positioned about 2cm (¾in) from one edge as shown in figure 4.

4 Iron the interfacing on the opposite side to the seam allowance and sew the short ends of the piece, taking a presser foot's seam allowance.

5 Turn right side out, slipstitch the opening closed and press.

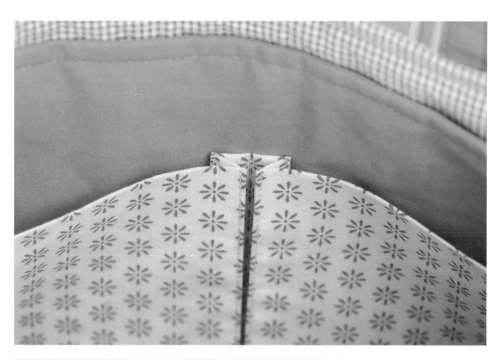

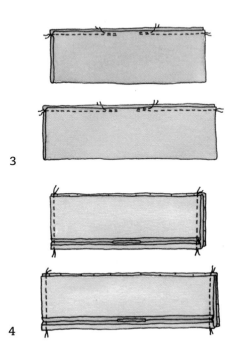

3

4

FOLDING ACCORDION PLEATS

Before pin tucks are sewn along the pleats, the accordion pocket can be positioned on an inner pocket. If the pocket is unexpectedly too wide or too narrow, you can adjust the pleats in the sides.

ADDING THE ACCORDION POCKET WITH TWO COMPARTMENTS

1 Mark the centre of the pocket with a pin.

2 Measure 1.5cm (⅝in) away from the middle and mark. Fold right sides together at your mark and press (see figure 5).

3 Measure 1.5cm (⅝in) away from the fold, mark and fold back the fabric at your mark (see figure 6).

4 Measure, mark, fold and press the pleat on the other side of the centre mark as just described to make a pleat in mirror image (see figure 7).

5 Turn the pocket fabric over and measure 3.5cm (1⅜in) away from the

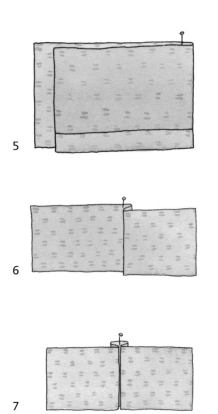

5

6

7

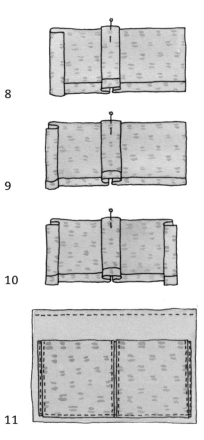

8

9

10

11

side. Mark, then fold and press the fabric in at your mark (see figure 8).

6 Measure 1.5cm (³⁄₈in) away from the fold. Mark, then fold and press the fabric at the mark (see figure 9).

7 Measure, mark, fold and press the pleat on the other side of the pocket in the same way (see figure 10).

8 Sew pin tucks 2mm (¹⁄₈in) from the folds on the front and back of the pocket.

9 Position the accordion pocket on an inner pocket piece, 0.5cm (¼in) from the sides and bottom edge.

10 Open the centre pleat and stitch in the middle between the pockets.

11 Sew the accordion pocket in place along the sides and bottom edge (see figure 11).

12 Set the pocket aside for later assembly.

ADDING THE ACCORDION POCKET WITH THREE COMPARTMENTS

1 Mark the centre of the pocket with a pin.

2 Turn the pocket wrong side up and mark half a pocket width as follows. For A4 size, measure 5cm (2in) away from the centre marking. For A3 size, measure 7.5cm (3in) away from the centre marking. Fold and press wrong sides together at the mark (see figure 12).

3 Measure 1.5cm (⅝in) away from the fold. Mark, fold and press the fabric in at the mark (see figure 13).

4 Turn the pocket over and measure 1.5cm (⅝in) away from the fold. Mark, fold and press the fabric at the mark (see figure 14).

5 Measure 1.5cm (⅝in) away from the fold. Mark, fold and press the fabric at the mark (see figure 15).

6 Turn the pocket over again and measure 3.5cm (1½in) away from the side. Mark, fold and press the fabric in at the mark (see figure 16).

7 Measure 1.5cm (⅝in) away from the fold. Mark, fold and press the fabric in at the mark (see figure 17).

8 Measure, mark, fold and press the pleat on the other side of the centre marking in the same way (see figure 18).

9 Sew pin tucks 2mm (¹⁄₈in) from the folds on the front and back of the pocket.

10 Position the pocket on an inner pocket, 0.5cm (¼in) from the sides and bottom edge.

11 Open the pleats and stitch in the middle between the pockets.

12 Sew the accordion pocket in place along the sides and bottom edge (see figure 19).

13 Put the pocket aside for later assembly.

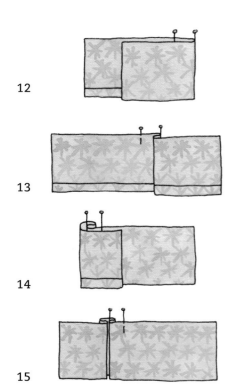

12

13

14

15

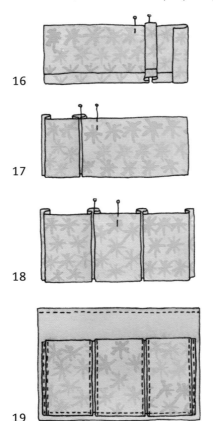

16

17

18

19

MAKING THE BAG BODY

1 Iron the volume fleece on to the wrong side of the fabric for the body.
2 Find the middle of the piece lengthways and mark the outside bottom edge of the bag. For A4 size, the bottom should be 7cm (2¾in) wide. For A3 size, the bottom should be 9cm (3½in) wide.

3 Mark the bottom on the inside. For A4 size, measure 4.25cm (1¾in) in from the ends of the piece. For A3 size, measure 5.25cm (2⅛in) in from the ends of the piece (see figure 1).
4 Centre the inner and outer pockets in position (see figure 1). Note which way up the pockets are facing in the diagram.
5 Sew the pockets in place along the sides and bottom edges.

MAKING THE HANDLE

1 Fold and press the handle fabric as shown in figure 2.
2 Open the fold and place the volume fleece in the middle of the fabric.
3 Put the short ends of the fabric right sides together and sew together, taking a pressure foot's seam allowance. Press the seam allowance open and fold the handle again.
4 Tack the handle and divide it into four (see figure 3).

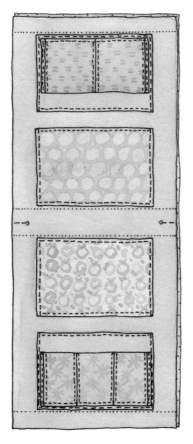

1

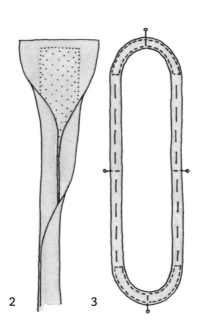

2   3

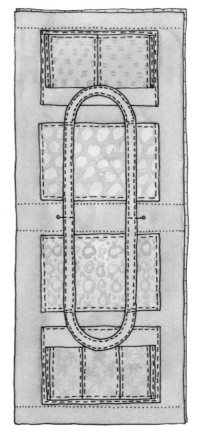

4

5 Topstitch the handle grips: for A4 size, sew 15.25cm (6in) on each side of opposite markers, so the grips measure 30.5cm (12in). For A3 size, sew 23cm (9in) on each side of opposite markers, so the grips measure 46cm (18in) as shown in figure 3.

6 Centre the handle's two quarter markings next to the middle of the bottom of the bag. For A4 size, measure 12.5cm (5in) in from the sides of the body. For A3 size, measure 16.5cm (6½in) in from the sides of the body.

7 Sew the handle in place (see figure 4).

8 Remove the tacking.

FINISHING THE INSIDE BOTTOM EDGE

1 Fold the bag right sides together and sew the ends together to be at the inside centre of the bag, taking a pressure foot's seam allowance. Press the seam allowance open.

2 Turn the bag right side out and position the seam just above the centre of the outside bottom.

3 Quilt the bottom and topstitch along the upper edges of the bag.

STITCHING THE SIDE PIN TUCKS

1 Sew marker stitches along both sides, as shown on the left of figure 5. For A4 size, sew the marker stitches 4.75cm (1⅞in) from the sides. For A3 size, sew them 6cm (2⅜in) from the sides.

2 Fold so that the marker stitches are lying just at the top of the fold.

3 Sew a pin tuck. For A4 size, sew the pin tuck 0.5cm (¼in) from the fold. For A3 size, sew the pin tuck 0.75cm (⁵⁄₁₆in) from the fold, as shown on the right of figure 5.

4 Sew a pin tuck in the other side as just described and remove the marker stitches.

FINISHING THE BAG

1 Shape the sides of the bag: for A4 size, insert pins on both sides 3.5cm (1⅜in) from the bottom centre fold; for A3 size, insert pins on both sides 4.5cm (1¾in) from the bottom centre fold.

2 Fold the bag outsides together around the pins so the bottom is inside the bag (see figure 7).

3 Fold the binding in half, wrong sides together. Press it and divide it into two equal lengths.

4 Sew the binding on both sides of the bag as described on page 9, figures 6a–6c.

5 Turn the finished back right side out.

5

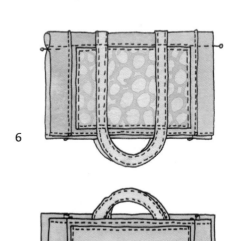

6

7

KNITTING BAG

This gorgeous bag is 38cm (15in) tall including handles, 28cm (11in) wide and 17cm (6¾in) deep, with pockets on each side. The large pockets on the sides have eight narrow compartments, each suitable for a pair of knitting needles, although you can make just one large pocket, if preferred. On both the ends are low pockets with compartments, suitable for crochet hooks, with a tall, narrow compartment behind them. The bag handles are large, strong knitting needles passed through four loops.

MATERIALS

Large pockets

Fabric, 16 strips	4.75 x 32.5cm (1¾ x 12¾in)
Lining, 2 pieces	27.25 x 32cm (10¾ x 12½in)
Volume fleece, 2 pieces	27.25 x 32cm (10¾ x 12½in)

Side pockets

Fabric, 8 strips	4.75 x 14cm (1¾ x 5½in)
Lining, 2 pieces	14.5 x 32cm (5¾ x 12½in)
Fabric, 2 pieces	14.5 x 44cm (5¾ x 17¼in)
Volume fleece, 2 pieces	14.5 x 44cm (5¾ x 17¼in)

Handle tabs

Fabric, 8 strips	4.75 x 9cm (1¾ x 3½in)
Lining and volume fleece, each	9.5 x 36cm (3¾ x 14in)

Main bag body

Fabric and lining, each	31 x 90cm (12¼ x 35½in)
Volume fleece, 2 pieces	31 x 90cm (12¼ x 35½in)
Fabric and lining for the ends, each	18.25 x 74cm (7¼ x 29in)
Volume fleece for the ends, 2 pieces	18.25 x 74cm (7¼ x 29in)
Binding	6.5 x 160cm (2½ x 63in)
2 knitting needles for handles	15mm (US size 19)

51

MAKING THE LARGE POCKETS

The large pockets are made from strips of fabric stitched together, but you can use a single piece of fabric with the same dimensions as the pocket lining, if preferred.

1 Place eight strips in the desired order.
2 Sew the strips together in pairs, right sides together.
3 Sew pairs right sides together and then join to form one piece with eight strips.
4 Press the seam allowances open and adjust the piece so the dimensions are 27.25 x 32cm (10¾ x 12½in).
5 Place the strip piece right sides together with the lining and place the volume fleece underneath.
6 Sew along all sides, leaving a 6cm (2⅜in) wide opening.
7 Cut the seam allowances off diagonally at the corners and turn right side out.

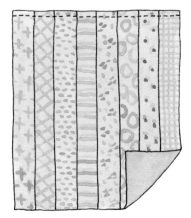

1

8 Press the pocket and slipstitch the opening closed.
9 Topstitch along the top edge of pocket (see figure 1).
10 Stitch another pocket the same way.
11 Set the pockets aside for later assembly.

MAKING THE END POCKETS

The low pockets on the ends are made from strips of fabric stitched together, but you can use a single piece of fabric with the dimensions of 14.5 x 13.5cm (5¾ x 5⅜in) if preferred.

1 Place four strips in the desired order.
2 Sew the strips together in pairs, right sides together.

3 Sew the pairs together right sides together, making a piece with four strips.
4 Press the seam allowances open and adjust the piece to the dimensions 14.5 x 13.5cm (5¾ x 5⅜in).
5 Sew the joined piece right sides together with the lining, making one oblong piece. Press the seam allowances open.
6 Put the piece right sides together with the fabric measuring 14.5 x 44cm (5¾ x 17¼in), and place the volume fleece underneath (see figure 2).
7 Sew along all sides, leaving a 6cm (2⅜in) wide opening.
8 Cut the seam allowances off diagonally at the corners and turn right side out.
9 Press the pocket and slipstitch the opening closed.
10 Fold the pocket so that the low pocket is 12cm (4¾in) tall and the tall pocket 30cm (12in) tall.
11 Topstitch along the upper edge of both pockets.
12 Sew along the seams between the strips (stitch in the ditch) so that narrow pockets are formed (see figure 3). When the pocket is attached to the side of the bag, the outer pockets will be closed.
13 Make a second set of end pockets the same way.
14 Set the pockets aside for later assembly.

MAKING THE TABS FOR THE HANDLES

1 Sew the strips for the handle tabs together in pairs.
2 Cut the lining and volume fleece into four pieces, each 9.5 x 9cm (3¾ x 3½in).
3 Place one joined fabric piece right sides together with a piece of lining and place the volume fleece underneath (see figure 4).
4 Sew together along both sides as shown on the left of figure 4.
5 Turn right side out and topstitch along the sides (see figure 5).
6 Sew in all four tabs the same way.
7 Set the tabs aside for later assembly.

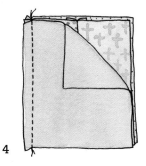

4

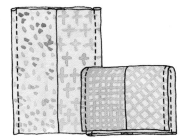

5

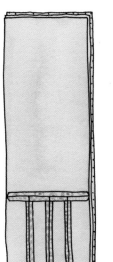

2

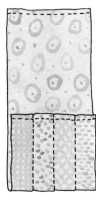

3

MAKING THE BAG BODY

The body of the bag is made as a rectangle that forms the front, back and bottom. The large pockets are stitched to this piece and then the ends are joined to the bag a little above the bottom. Finally, the pockets are sewn on the two ends.

1 Iron the volume fleece to the wrong side of both the fabric and the lining for the bag.

2 Fold the tabs in half and position two on each of the short edges, placing them 2.75cm (1in) in from the long edges (see figure 6).

3 Place the fabric and the lining right sides together and sew the short edges together.

4 Turn right side out and press; topstitch along the newly stitched edges.

5 Mark the centre of the long edges and then mark the bottom by measuring 9cm (3½in) from each side of the centre marking.

6 Topstitch across the bag between the markings.

7 Centre a large pocket 4.25cm (1¾in) below each edge with the tabs.

8 Sew the pockets in place along the sides and the bottom (see figure 7).

9 Sew down the seam lines between the strips (stitch in the ditch) to make the narrow pockets – you can do this on one of the pockets or on both.

PREPARING THE END PIECES

1 Iron the volume fleece to the wrong side of the fabric and lining for the ends.

2 Cut the fabric and lining into two pieces, each 18.25 x 37cm (7¼ x 14½in).

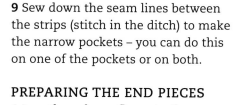

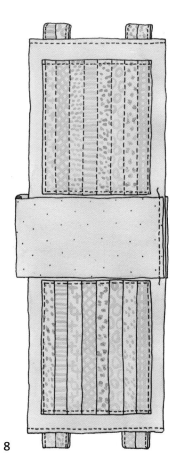

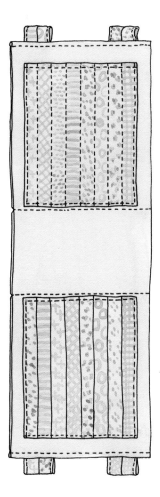

6

7

8

3 Place a piece of fabric and lining right sides together and sew one short edge together.
4 Turn right side out, press and topstitch the sewn edge.

FINISHING THE BAG

1 Place one end piece right sides together with the body at the position of the bag bottom.
2 Fold the lining side, which is lying on top, behind and under the body (see figure 8).

3 Sew with a presser foot's seam allowance and turn right side out.
4 Centre an end pocket 4.25cm (1¾in) from the top edge.
5 Sew the pocket in place along the sides and bottom edge (see figure 9).
6 Attach the other end piece and its pocket in the same way.
7 Fold the bag right sides together as shown in figure 10 to match one side panel to the adjacent end panel.
8 Divide the binding strip into four pieces, each 6.5 x 40cm (2½ x 15¾in).
9 Sew the binding to each of the four vertical side seams of the bag, as described on page 9, figures 6a–6c, refolding the bag as in step 7 to match each seam as you go.
10 Turn right side out and slide the knitting needles in the tabs.

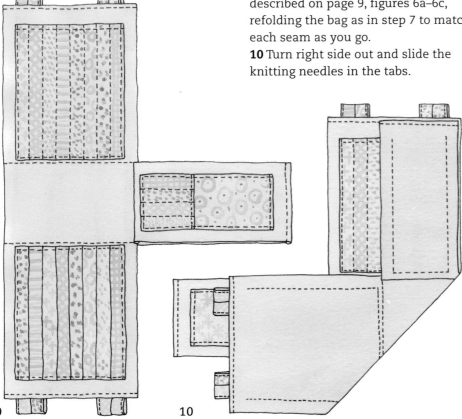

9

10

55

ZIGZAGS

The zigzag is an easy pattern but the variations are wide ranging and lend themselves well to experimenting with different patterned fabrics. How clearly the zigzag pattern is seen is determined by the choice of fabric patterns and colours.

The materials for each of the four variations here are suitable for the front of a 40 x 40cm (16 x 16in) cushion cover. Instructions for making the cushion are on page 60.

MATERIALS

Two–fabric zigzags

Fabric colour A, 18 squares	9.25 x 9.25cm (3⁵/₈ x 3 ⁵/₈in)
Fabric colour B, 18 squares	9.25 x 9.25cm (3⁵/₈ x 3⁵/₈in)

Thick and thin zigzags

Fabric in various colours, 24 squares	9.25 x 9.25cm (3⁵/₈ x 3⁵/₈in)
Fabric in the 'base' colour, 12 squares	9.25 x 9.25cm (3⁵/₈ x 3⁵/₈in)

Five zigzag bands

Fabric in 6 different colours, 6 squares, each	9.25 x 9.25cm (3⁵/₈ x 3⁵/₈in)

Repeated zigzag

Fabric colour A, 12 squares	9.25 x 9.25cm (3⁵/₈ x 3⁵/₈in)
Fabric colour B, 12 squares	9.25 x 9.25cm (3⁵/₈ x 3⁵/₈in)
Fabric colour C, 12 squares	9.25 x 9.25cm (3⁵/₈ x 3⁵/₈in)

TWO-FABRIC ZIGZAGS

THICK AND THIN ZIGZAGS

FIVE ZIGZAG BANDS

REPEATED ZIGZAG

TWO-FABRIC ZIGZAG

1 Place each square in colour A right sides together with a square in colour B.
2 Sew the squares diagonally and then cut them in half as described on page 11, figures 10a–10d.
3 Arrange the two-coloured squares as shown in figure 1.
4 Sew the squares together to form a piece of patchwork as described opposite (see 'Zigzag Patchwork').

THICK AND THIN ZIGZAG

The fabric pieces for this design are the same size as in the previous example, but the 'thin' zigzags are made from one fabric, which we can call the base fabric, while the 'thick' bands are made from a variety of fabrics – nine in the example shown.

1 Place 12 squares of different colours right sides together in pairs. Lay them out with the most possible combinations.
2 Place the other 12 squares of different colours right sides together in pairs with 12 squares of 'base' colour.
3 Sew the squares diagonally and then cut them in half as described on page 11, figures 10a–10d.
4 Arrange the two-coloured squares as shown in figure 2 (the 'base' colour is shown in pale pink).
5 Sew the squares together to form a piece of patchwork as described opposite (see 'Zigzag Patchwork').

FIVE ZIGZAG BANDS

This arrangement is stitched with six different fabrics. Five fabrics form five zigzag lines and the sixth fabric forms the 'base', filling in the background areas along the top and bottom edges to complete the square.

1 Pair up the squares as shown in figure 3 and then pin them right sides together. Make three pairs of each combination.
2 Sew the squares diagonally and then cut them in half as described on page 11, figures 10a–10d.
3 Arrange the two-coloured squares as shown in figure 4.
4 Sew the squares together to form a piece of patchwork as described opposite (see 'Zigzag Patchwork').

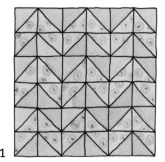

1

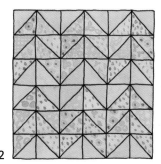

2

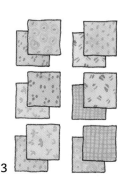

3

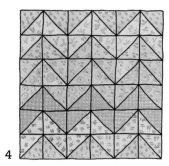

4

REPEATED ZIGZAG

In this example, the zigzag pattern is formed from three fabric colour groups: A, B and C. Group C is cut from seven different patterned fabrics.

1 Pair up the squares as shown in figure 5 and then pin them right sides together. Make six pairs of each.

2 Sew the squares diagonally and then cut them in half as described on page 11, figures 10a–10d.

3 Arrange the two-coloured squares as shown in figure 6.

4 Sew the squares together to form a piece of zigzag patchwork as described next.

ZIGZAG PATCHWORK

The 36 half square triangle units are sewn together as follows. Press the seam allowances open as you go.

1 Place the squares from two vertical rows right sides together and sew together in pairs (see figure 7).

2 Sew the resulting pairs right sides together into blocks as shown in figure 8.

3 Sew the blocks together into a strip (see figure 9).

4 Join two more strips in the same way (see figure 10).

5 Stitch the strips together into one piece (see figure 11).

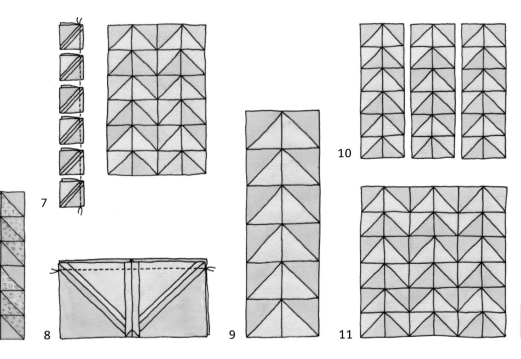

5   6   7   8   9   10   11

ZIGZAG CHAIR CUSHIONS

Zigzag patchwork is perfect for square chair cushions. The simple method of construction given here means that the cover cannot be removed easily for washing, so you will need a cushion pad that can be washed with the cover. Alternatively, you can make the back of the cushion cover following the instructions for the butterfly cushion on page 85 so that it can be removed. The stitch pattern for the quilting is on page 117.

MAKING THE CUSHION COVER

1 Place the volume fleece and the lining fabric under the zigzag patchwork and tack the layers together.
2 Stitch along the zigzag seam lines (stitch in the ditch) as shown in figure 1. Alternatively, quilt in a flower pattern using tear-away stabiliser as described on page 9, figure 3 and as shown here in figure 2. Use the pattern on page 117.
3 Use marker stitches to mark a 20cm (8in) opening on one edge of the patchwork piece and backing fabric.
4 Place the patchwork right sides together with the backing fabric and sew together along all sides, leaving the marked opening free.
5 Turn right side out and insert the cushion into the cover.
6 Slipstitch the opening closed and remove any visible marker stitching.
7 Make hand stitches right through the cover and cushion in four places as shown in figure 3. Tie the thread ends together with a strong knot.

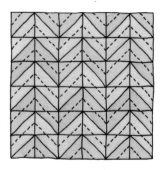

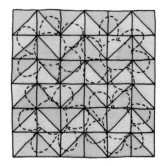

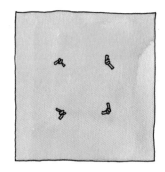

1   2   3

MATERIALS

Zigzag patchwork (see previous pages)	41.5 x 41.5cm (16½ x 16¼in)
Volume fleece	41.5 x 41.5cm (16½ x 16¼in)
Fabric for lining	41.5 x 41.5cm (16½ x 16¼in))
Tear-away stabiliser (optional)	18 x 90cm (7 x 35½in)
Fabric for backing (cushion back)	41.5 x 41.5cm (16½ x 16¼in)
Chair cushion pad	40 x 40cm (16 x 16in)

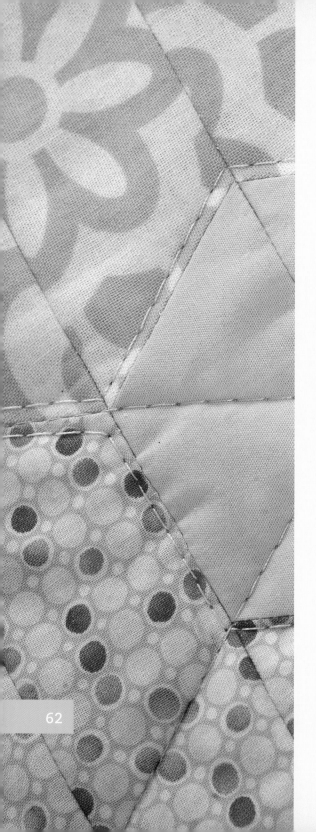

HEXAGONS

Using the method described here, hexagons can be sewn together on the sewing machine. Half hexagons – which are referred to as trapezia here – are sewn together in rows, and when two rows are joined, the hexagons will become visible. The rows can be stitched in horizontal or vertical rows.

You can buy quilting rulers and templates for cutting hexagons or draw up an exact pattern on technical grid paper with a triangular pattern. The patterns for the regular hexagons and elongated hexagons used in this book are provided on pages 118 and 119. To make a pattern for the half hexagons, see the instructions below. For information on how to join the trapezia into hexagons, see the project starting on page 64.

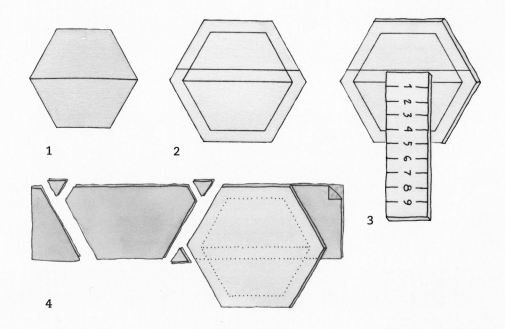

1

2

3

4

MAKING A TEMPLATE FOR A HALF HEXAGON

1 Draw a hexagon on grid paper in the desired finished size and draw the hexagon's horizontal bisecting axis (see figure 1).

2 Draw a seam allowance around the whole hexagon and to the side of the bisector (see figure 2).

3 Transfer the drawing to firm template plastic or glue the drawing on to heavy cardboard.

4 Check your pattern is level and cut out the full hexagon.

CUTTING THE FABRIC

The reason for using a whole hexagon as a template is that it is easy to hold in place when cutting. For convenience, half hexagons are called trapezia in the steps which follow.

1 Measure the template as shown in figure 3. The measurement determines the width of the fabric strip.

2 Cut strips to your measurement – using a rotary cutter, you can cut through several layers of fabric at once if desired.

3 Place the template on one or more fabric strips, so the seam allowance line along the hexagon's bisector follows the edge of the strip/strips.

4 Cut trapezia as shown in figure 4. Trim off the small corners, as shown, to make sewing the trapezia together easier.

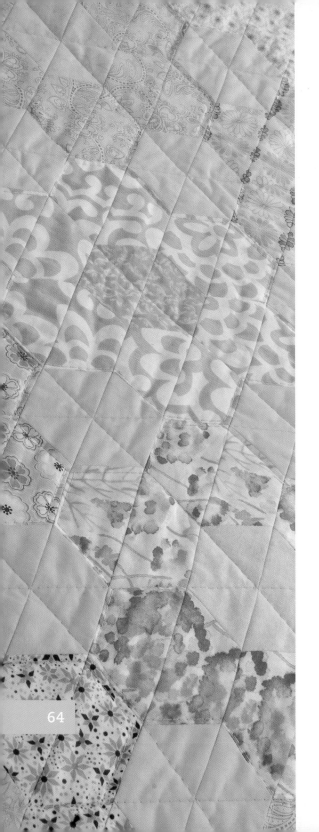

HEXAGON QUILTS

For these quilts, the trapezia, or half hexagons, are sewn together in vertical and horizontal rows. When the rows are joined, the trapezia form hexagons. For either quilt it is a good idea to lay out all the cut-out pairs of trapezia on a sheet or similar before you begin stitching, both to keep an eye on the distribution and to keep order in the rows when they are joined. Find a system that is logical and sew one row at a time. When sewing vertical columns, it is easiest to work from the top down, so the top two trapezia in the outermost row to the left are sewn together first.

MATERIALS FOR GRANDMOTHER'S FLOWERBED

Section A (6 required)

Fabric for petals, 6 different designs	5 x 115cm (2 x 45¼in)
Fabric for flower centres, 6 different designs	5 x 21cm (2 x 8¼in)
Fabric for the spaces or leaves	5 x 260cm (2 x 102½in)

Section B (5 required)

Fabric for petals, 6 different designs	5 x 115cm (2 x 45¼in)
Fabric for flower centres, 6 different designs	5 x 21cm (2 x 8¼in)
Fabric for spaces/leaves	5 x 260cm (2 x 102½in)

Edging and assembly

Fabric for edging, 2 pieces	5 x 205cm (2 x 80¾in)
Fabric for backing	140 x 205cm (55 x 80¾in)
Quilt wadding	140 x 205cm (55 x 80¾in)

MATERIALS FOR THE WATER'S EDGE

Two rows of trapezia (31 required)

Fabric	6.25 x 250cm (2½ x 98½in)

Assembly

Fabric for backing	110 x 155cm (43¼ x 61in)
Quilt wadding	110 x 155cm (43¼ x 61in)

GRANDMOTHER'S FLOWERBED

This pretty, traditional-style quilt is 130 x 195cm (51¼ x 76¾in). The trapezia or half hexagons from which the quilt is made are joined together in vertical columns to create 66 flowers, each made up of six petal shapes and a flower centre. There are also 132 hexagonal spaces, which could suggest leaves. The petals are cut from 24 different fabrics, the flower centres from eight different colours, and all the spaces or leaves are one fabric colour. The design uses the small regular hexagon pattern on page 118.

There are several ways to position the flowers. Here, they are laid out in two sets, each creating a row of flowers. This way the flowers are staggered in the two formations, A and B. You will need six of group A and five of group B. For the sake of clarity, the materials list provides quantities for one group A and one group B. From this, it is possible to calculate and design a quilt to your own specifications.

CUTTING AND ARRANGING THE PIECES

1 Cut six pairs of trapezia for each flower's petals and one pair of trapezia for each flower centre. For the quilt shown you will need a total of 66 sets of petals and 66 flower centres, along with 132 pairs of trapezia for spaces.
2 Arrange the flowers (petals and centres) and spaces (or leaves) on a sheet to assess the colour distribution (see the illustration).

A

B

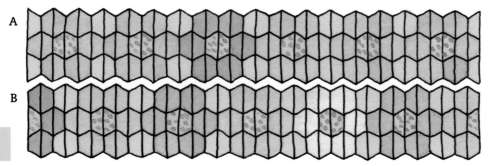

JOINING THE TRAPEZIA IN VERTICAL COLUMNS

Having laid out the pieces you can now proceed to stitch them together in vertical columns, starting at the top-left corner of the arrangement.

1 Place two trapezia right sides together and sew together (see figure 2). Press the seam allowances open.
2 Repeat to sew the entire column of trapezia together in pairs.
3 Sew the pairs together to join the whole column (see figure 3).
4 Sew all the columns in the same way.
5 Join two columns together (see figure 4).
6 Repeat to join all the columns together in pairs.
7 Sew the resulting columns together into one piece (see figure 5) – when

joining two joined columns to another two joined columns, sew from the other end in order to avoid the piece being pulled out of shape.

ADDING THE EDGING STRIPS

1 Sew an edging strip to one side of the piece (see the photograph on page 66).
2 Press the seam allowances open and trim both ends of the strip to the hexagon template.
3 Sew the second edging strip on to the other side of the piece and trim it in the same way.

ASSEMBLING THE QUILT

1 Use marker stitching to mark a 30cm (12in) opening along one straight edge of the patchwork.

2 Place the patchwork wrong side down on the quilt wadding and roughly tack the layers together.
3 Trim the quilt wadding to the exact shape of the patchwork.
4 Place the backing fabric right sides together with the patchwork and sew the layers together, except across the marked opening.
5 Trim the backing fabric to shape and cut notches in the seam allowance between the points for ease.
6 Turn the quilt right side out and slipstitch the opening closed.
7 Tack the quilt layers together and quilt stitch it, perhaps stitching in the ditch around the hexagons or creating larger diamond shapes.
8 Remove the tacking threads.

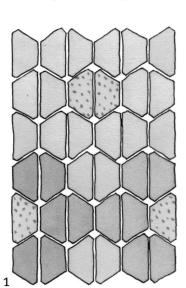

1

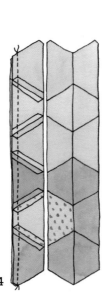

2

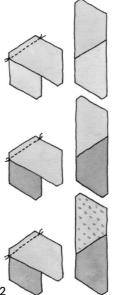

3

4

5

WATER'S EDGE QUILT

This pretty quilt is 102 x 145cm (40 x 57in). This time, the trapezia are stitched together in horizontal rows to create 180 full hexagons plus 12 halves. About 35 different fabrics are used, positioned in a random, but harmonious, order. The quilt uses the large regular hexagon pattern on page 119.

Each strip is 6.25cm (2½in) wide, and you should cut as many as possible from each chosen fabric.

The materials list on page 64 indicates the fabric required for two rows of trapezia (see figure 1).

CUTTING AND ARRANGING THE PIECES

1 Cut 186 pairs of trapezia.
2 On a sheet or similar, arrange the pieces in 31 horizontal rows with 12 trapezia in each row, so colour distribution and direction can be assessed.

JOINING THE TRAPEZIA IN HORIZONTAL ROWS

1 Place the trapezia from the top row right sides together in pairs and sew as shown in figure 2. Press the seam allowances open.

2 Join the pairs right sides together for the whole row in the same way (see figures 3 and 4).
3 Stitch the rows together as shown in figure 5. When stitching two joined rows to another two other joined rows, sew from the other end in order to avoid the piece being pulled out of shape.
4 When the quilt top is the desired size, complete the quilt as explained in 'Assembling the Quilt', page 67.

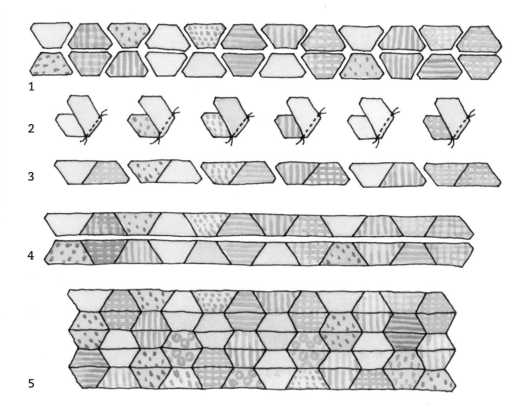

1

2

3

4

5

HEXAGON CUSHIONS

If you can imagine a regular hexagon being pulled a little on two opposite sides, the result is a tall hexagon, which is used here to make two cushion covers. Although the cushions use the same pattern, the placement of colours produces two completely different looks. The finished cushions are 35 x 62cm (13¾ x 24½in). The pattern for the tall hexagon is on page 118.

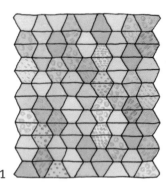

1

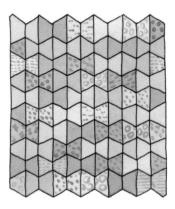

2

CHINESE-LANTERNS CUSHION
For this cushion cover, join pairs of tall trapezia together in horizontal rows. Matching fabrics meet along the broad side of the trapezia in shapes reminiscent of Chinese lanterns.

1 Create a pattern for the trapezium or half hexagon following the instructions on pages 62–63 and using

the tall hexagon from page 118. Cut four pairs of trapezia from each of 14 fabrics or a total of 54 pairs of tall trapezia.

2 Lay the pairs out in horizontal rows as shown in figure 1.

3 Sew the trapezia together in horizontal rows (see page 68).

4 Complete the cushion following 'Assembling the Cover' on page 72.

MATERIALS	
Fabrics, 14 different, each	7.5 x 85cm (3 x 33½in)
Volume fleece	67 x 74.5cm (26½ x 29¼in)
Fabric for lining	67 x 82cm (26½ x 32¼in)
Velcro tapes, 2cm (¾in) wide	34cm (13½in)
Fabric for binding, 2 pieces	6.5 x 37.5cm (2½ x 14¾in)

BOW-PATTERNED CUSHION

In this variation, the trapezia pairs are laid out with their short sides towards each other. This produces a new shape, which looks like a bow. The trapezia pairs are sewn together in vertical columns.

1 Create a pattern for the trapezium or half hexagon following the instructions on pages 62–63 and using the tall hexagon from page 118. Cut four pairs from each of 14 fabrics or a total of 55 pairs of tall trapezia.
2 Lay the pairs out in vertical columns as shown in figure 2 on page 70.
3 Sew the trapezia together in vertical columns as described on page 67 and then join the rows.
4 Trim the tips off at both ends of the patchwork piece to make a neat rectangle.
5 Complete the cushion following 'Assembling the Cover', below.

ASSEMBLING THE COVER

1 Iron the volume fleece on to the patchwork piece so that it follows a straight edge: on the Chinese lanterns patchwork this means along the side that measures 65cm (25½in); on the bow-patterned piece this means along one side on which the tips have been cut off, measuring 67cm (26½in). At the opposite end, the volume fleece should be 2.5cm (1in) longer.

2 Place the lining right sides together with the patchwork piece, so it follows the straight edge and the volume fleece. At the opposite end, the lining fabric should be 10cm (4in) longer.
3 Sew the layers together at the matched end (see figure 3).
4 Turn right side out, tack the layers together roughly and quilt the piece as desired.
5 Fold a double hem on the lining as shown in figure 4.
6 Tack the hem.
7 Adjust the piece at the sides, making it 62cm (24½in) wide.
8 Centre one part of the Velcro tape along the edge of the lining side of the overlap.
9 Sew the tape in place with two lines of stitching.
10 Centre and sew the other part of the Velcro tape on the hem edge as shown in figures 5 and 6.
11 Press the Velcro tapes together and sew the side edges of the cover.
12 Turn the lining right side out.
13 Attach binding to both sides of the cover as described on page 9, figures 6a–6c.

3
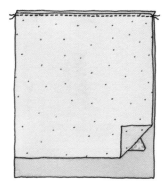

4
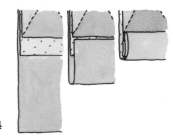

5

6
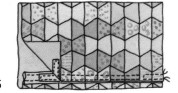

MATERIALS

Fabrics, 14 different, each	7.5 x 85cm (3 x 33½in)
Volume fleece	67 x 75cm (26½ x 29½in)
Fabric for lining	67 x 82.5cm (26½ x 32½in)
Velcro tapes, 2cm (¾in) wide	34cm (13½in)
Fabric for binding, 2 pieces	6.5 x 37.5cm (2½ x 14¾in)

BUCKET BAGS

This versatile bag will fold down flat when the lining is pulled out, making it easy to store when not in use. The small bag is 19cm (7½in) tall with a 15 x 15cm (6 x 6in) base and a circumference at the top of 64cm (25in). It has a top closure formed by two handmade buttons and a fabric loop. The large bag is 26cm (10¼in) tall with a 20 x 20cm (8 x 8in) base and a circumference at the top of 80cm (31½in). This bag can be used as a storage basket.

Each bag can be sewn from different fabrics so it will have a top border and a lining that are different from the outside and, of course, the button closure and tab of the small bag can use different fabrics too. As a variation, the large bag can have one of two patchwork designs for the outside section (see pages 78–79). The fabric is quilted on insulated wadding because this provides good support. The seam allowances are tacked in place on the insulated material before the bag is turned right side out.

MATERIALS

Size	Small	Large
Fabric for the outside	27 x 66cm (10½ x 26in)	36 x 85.5cm (14¼ x 33¾in)
Fabric for the lining	27 x 66cm (10½ x 26in)	36 x 85.5cm (14¼ x 33¾in)
Fabric for the edging	8 x 66cm (3¼ x 26in)	8 x 85.5cm (3¼ x 33¾in)
Insulated wadding	59 x 66cm (23¼ x 26in)	77 x 85.5cm (30¼ x 33¾in)
Buttons	2	
Fabric strap	8 x 38cm (3¼ x 15in)	
Volume fleece for the strap	2 x 36cm (¾ x14¼in)	

Large bag with hour-glass pattern

Fabrics, 6 different, each	7.5 x 100cm (3 x 39½in)
Fabric for the bottom and side	15 x 85.5cm (6 x 33¾in)
Fabric for the lining	40 x 85.5cm (15¾ x 33¾in)
Insulated wadding	77 x 85.5cm (30¼ x 33¾in)

Large bag with bow pattern

Fabrics, 11 different, each	5.75 x 90cm (2¼ x 35½in)
Fabric for the bottom and side	13.5 x 85.5cm (5 3/8 in x 33¾in)
Fabric for the edging	8.5 x 85.5cm (3 3/8 x 33¾in)
Fabric for the lining	35 x 85.5cm (13¾ x 33¾in)
Insulated wadding	77 x 85.5cm (30¼ x 33¾in)

BOTH BAGS: GETTING STARTED

1 Sew the edging fabric between the outer fabric and the lining as shown in figure 1 with right sides facing and raw edges matching.

2 Place the wrong side of the fabric against the insulated wadding and quilt the layers.

3 Trim the piece so the edges are straight and at right angles. Sew around the piece with a stitch length of 1.5 to prevent the quilting stitches from coming loose.

SMALL BAG: BUTTONS

1 Sew two buttons (see page 26).

2 Measure 8.5cm (3⅜in) from one edge and mark the position of a button 1.5cm (⅝in) down from the edging strip.

3 Mark the position of another button 31.5cm (12½in) from the first marking and 1.5cm (⅝in) down from the edging strip.

4 Sew the buttons in place on the markings (see figure 2).

BOTH BAGS: SHAPING THE BAG

1 Fold the piece with right sides together, lining to lining and quilted fabric to quilted fabric, to make a long tube bisected horizontally by the edging strip.

2 Mark a 12cm (4¾in) opening on the lining side of the long edge, 4cm (1½in) from the edging strip.

3 Sew the seam, except across the opening. Press the seam allowances open and tack them in place on the wadding.

4 Divide the tube into four at one end and mark with pins (see figure 3).

5 Fold pleats, bringing the pins together in the centre (see figure 4).

6 Place the patchwork ruler as shown in figure 5 and trim off the corners.

7 Fold two corners right sides together and sew together (see figure 6).

8 Press the seam allowances open and tack them in place on the insulated wadding.

9 Fold so that the corners you have just sewn are positioned in the middle and sew the remaining edges of the base together (see figure 7).

10 Divide, fold pleats, cut and sew the opposite end of the tube in the same way.

11 Turn the bag right side out and sew up the opening with slipstitch.

12 Stuff the lining down into the outer side.

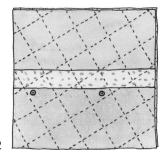

1

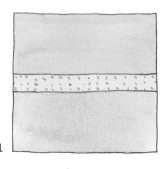

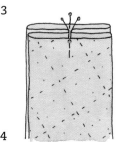

2

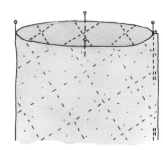

3

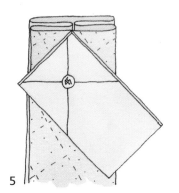

4

5

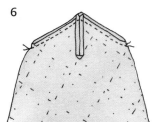

6

7

SMALL BAG: STRAP

1 Fold and press the strap fabric (see figure 8). Open the fold and iron the volume fleece in the middle of the fabric strip.

2 Fold the strap and insert pins (see figure 9), noting that you will need to allow for seam allowances where the two ends of the strap fabric meet.

3 Open the fold at the ends, sew them together with right sides facing and press the seam allowances open.

4 Fold the strap again and sew 2mm (1/16in) from the open edge, taking the pins out as you go along and stretching out the strap when sewing past the tips.

5 Fold and press the tips of the strap and put the strap around the buttons.

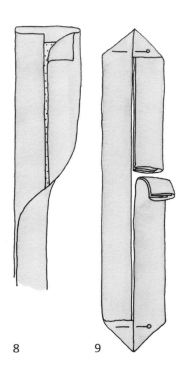

8   9

LARGE BAG WITH HOUR-GLASS PATTERN

The outside of this lovely storage bag is a patchwork of large, tall hexagons, the pattern for which is on page 118. The patchwork is 25 x 85.5cm (10 x 33¾in). The tall pairs of trapezia are laid out in horizontal rows with the short sides together.
This produces shapes that look like hour glasses.

1 Cut four or five pairs of trapezia from each fabric to make up a total of 24 pairs.
2 Lay out the pairs in four horizontal rows with 12 tall trapezia in each row, as shown in figure 10.
3 Sew the trapezia together as described on page 68. The finished patchwork piece measures 25 x 85.5cm (10 x 33¾in).

ASSEMBLING THE LARGE BAG WITH HOUR-GLASS PATTERN

1 Sew the patchwork piece right sides together with the fabric for the bottom, matching the 85.5cm (33¾in) edges, and press the seam allowances on to the bottom fabric.
2 Sew the lining fabric right sides together with the other side of the patchwork piece and press the seam allowances on to the lining fabric (see figure 11).
3 Place the insulated wadding underneath the piece and roughly tack the layers together.
4 Quilt the piece.
5 Cut the tips off at both sides and sew around the piece to prevent the quilting stitches from coming undone, using a stitch length of 1.5.
6 Sew the basket together as described on page 76, figures 3–7.

LARGE BAG WITH BOW PATTERN

This handy storage bag features a patchwork of small, tall hexagons, the pattern for which is on page 118. The pairs of tall trapezia are laid out in vertical columns with the short sides together. This produces shapes that look like bows. The patchwork is 24.5 x 85.5cm (9¾ x 33¾in).

1 Cut five or six pairs of tall trapezia from each fabric to make up a total of 60 pairs.
2 Lay out the pairs in 20 vertical columns with six tall trapezia in each one (see figure 12).
3 Sew the trapezia together as described on page 67.
4 Cut the tips off at the top and bottom edges so that the piece measures 24.5 x 85.5cm (9¾ x 33¾in).

ASSEMBLING THE LARGE BAG WITH BOW PATTERN

1 Sew the patchwork piece right sides together with the fabric for the bottom, matching the 85.5cm (33¾in) edges, and press the seam allowances on to the bottom fabric.
2 Sew the edging fabric right sides together with the other side of the patchwork piece and press the seam allowances on to the edging fabric.
3 Sew the lining fabric right sides together with the other side of the edging fabric and press the seam allowance on to the lining fabric (see figure 13).

10

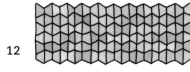

12

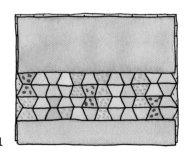

11

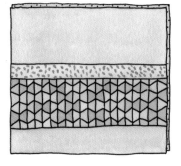

13

4 Place the insulated wadding underneath the piece and roughly tack the layers together.
5 Quilt the piece.

6 Sew around the edge of the piece with a stitch length of 1.5 to prevent the quilting stitches from coming undone.
7 Sew the basket together as described on page 76, figures 3–7.

BUTTERFLIES

This interesting design is a development of the half hexagon or trapezium pattern used for the previous projects. When two trapezia are stitched together on the short edges with a narrow strip of fabric in between, they transform into a butterfly. Small fabric triangles fill the spaces – the air or background behind the butterflies – at each end.

The finished butterfly panel is 15 x 15cm (6 x 6in), a versatile size that can be used for cushions or even full quilts (see page 86). Patterns for the wings and background triangles are provided on page 119.

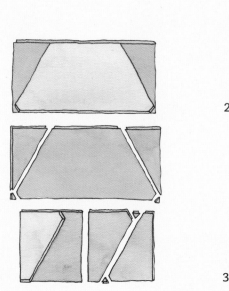

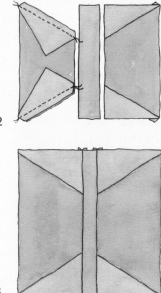

1

2

3

MATERIALS

Per butterfly

Fabric for the wings	7.5 x 32cm (3 x 12⅝in)
Fabric for the background triangles	7.5 x 11cm (3 x 4⅜in)
Fabric for the body strip	3.5 x 15cm (1½ x 6in)

BUTTERFLY PANEL

1 Fold the fabrics for the wings and the background right sides together and cut out one wing and two background triangles (see figure 1).

2 Place two background triangles right sides together with a wing and sew together (see figure 2).

3 Make a second wing section in the same way.

4 Press the seam allowances open (see figure 2).

5 Place the body strip right sides together with a wing section and sew together. Repeat to join the second wing section to the other side of the body strip (see figure 3).

6 Press the seam allowances open.

7 Trim the patchwork so that the butterfly measures 15 x 15cm (6 x 6in).

8 Repeat to make the required number of butterflies.

BUTTERFLY CUSHIONS

There are three designs to choose from here. The simplest version has a single butterfly on the front (option A). The other two designs both feature four butterflies, but one has a frame around each of the four butterflies (option B) and the other simply has the framing around the panel of four (option C). All three designs have a wide border around the patchwork panel.

All the cushions fit a 40 x 40cm (16 x 16in) cushion pad. The pattern for the floral quilt stitching is given on page 117.

MATERIALS

Design option	A	B	C
Butterfly panel(s)	1	4	4
Fabric for the bars			3.5 x 65cm
			(1³/₈ x 25½in)
Fabric for the frame border	3.5 x 70cm	3.5 x 125cm	3.5 x 140cm
	(1³/₈ x 27½in)	(1³/₈ x 49¼in)	(1³/₈ x 55in)
Fabric for the outside border	13.25 x 130cm	6.75 x 155cm	5.75 x 155cm
	(5¼ x 51¼in)	(2¾ x 61in)	(2¼ x 61in)

Additional materials

Wadding/volume fleece	42 x 42cm (16½ x 16½in)
Fabric for the lining	42 x 42cm (16½ x 16½in)
Tear-away stabiliser (option B only)	18 x 90cm (7 x 35½in)
Fabric for the back, 2 pieces	28 x 42cm (11 x 16½in)
3 buttons, 3 press studs or Velcro tapes	2.5 x 31cm (1 x 12¼in)
Binding	6.5 x 175cm (2½ x 69in)
Cushion pad	40 x 40cm (16 x 16in)

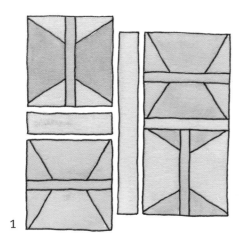

1

MAKING THE BUTTERFLY PATCHWORK

1 Make the chosen number of butterfly panels – one for option A and four for options B and C.

2 For option C, join the butterflies together into one panel. The butterflies can either face in the same direction or be rotated a quarter turn relative to each other. Alternatively, for option B, stitch the four butterflies with the dividing bars between them (see figure 1).

FRAMING THE BUTTERFLIES

1 Place a narrow framing strip right sides together with the patchwork piece. The strip should extend one border width beyond the patchwork piece. Sew as shown in figure 2.

2 Trim the strip to length so it follows the next edge. Press the border outwards.

3 Place a new border strip right sides together with the next side and sew together as shown in figure 3. Trim the strip to length and press the border outwards as before.

4 Sew border strips right sides together on the third and fourth sides in the same way.

5 Fold the border strip sewn first right sides together with the one sewn last, as shown in figure 4, and complete the sewing of the first border strip.

6 Press the seam allowances and the border outwards (see figure 5).

7 Sew a wide border around the bordered patchwork piece in the same way (see figure 6).

8 Trim the fabric to make a piece 42 x 42cm (16½ x 16½in).

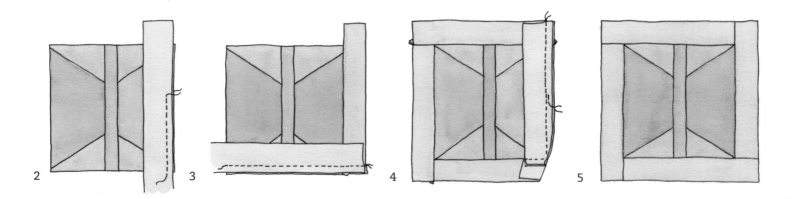

2 3 4 5

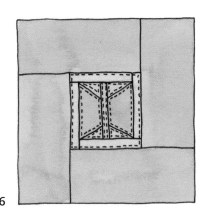

6

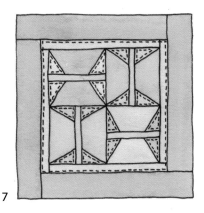

7

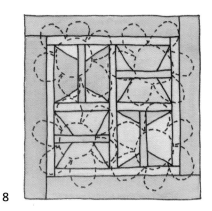

8

QUILTING THE PATCHWORK

1 Place the patchwork piece with the wrong side down on the wadding. Place the lining fabric underneath, again with the wrong side against the wadding, and tack the layers together.
2 Quilt the patchwork following the quilt pattern shown in figures 6, 7 or 8, depending on which option you are making. For option B, use tear-away stabiliser as described on page 9, figure 3, and shown here in figure 8. The pattern for the flower is on page 117.

ASSEMBLING THE BACK

The back is made from two identical pieces that are attached so that there is a 3cm (1¼in) overlap. The opening at the overlap can be closed with buttons and buttonholes, press studs or Velcro tape.

1 Fold a hem along one 42cm (16½in) edge of each back piece – first turn 1cm (³⁄₈in) and then 3cm (1¼in) as shown in figure 9.
2 Decide on the method of closing and attach the Velcro, press studs or buttons with buttonholes: press studs or buttons and buttonholes should be sewn 1.5cm (³⁄₈in) from the folded edge; for Velcro, place the tape on the front and back respectively of the hem edge as shown in figure 10.
3 Button or fasten the pieces together and sew on each side of the opening (see left side of figure 10).
4 Place the front piece right sides together with the back piece.
5 Sew the pieces together along the four sides and zigzag the raw edges together. Alternatively, sew on binding, as described on page 9, figures 6a–6c.

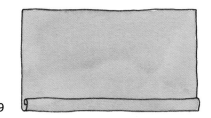

9

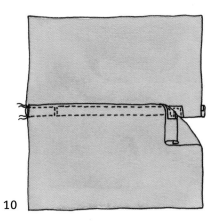

10

BUTTERFLY QUILT

This splendid quilt is made using the same butterfly as featured on the cushions on page 82. It measures 127 x 180cm (50 x 71in) with 77 butterflies in seven vertical rows and eleven horizontal rows. The joined butterflies are framed by a narrow border and then a wide border and the backing fabric (which is the same fabric as was used for the narrow border in the quilt shown) is folded into an edge that is visible on the front.

BUTTERFLY PATCHWORK

1 Cut and sew 77 butterfly panels following the instructions on pages 80–81.

2 Stitch the butterflies together in 11 horizontal rows with seven butterflies on each row.

3 Press the seam allowances open.

4 Sew the rows together, press the seam allowances open and, if necessary, trim the seam allowances.

5 Sew a narrow border and then a wide border around the piece as shown in figure 1 – stitch a border strip on to each end first with right sides facing and then stitch the borders to the sides.

QUILTING THE LAYERS

1 Place the wadding underneath. Trim the wadding to the same size as the patchwork piece and tack the layers together roughly.

2 Centre the patchwork on the backing fabric and tack the layers together ready for quilting.

3 Quilt the piece and tie the thread ends with a quilting knot (see page 9, figure 4).

ATTACHING THE BACKING

1 Trim the backing fabric so that it is 5cm (2in) wider than the patchwork piece all round.

2 Fold and press the edges as shown in figures 2 and 3.

3 Open the fold and trim off the corners as shown in figure 4.

4 Fold the corners and edges as shown in figure 5.

5 Sew down the folded edge on the sewing machine or hand sew with slipstitches.

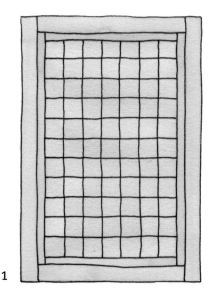

1

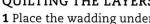

MATERIALS	
Fabric for wings and small triangles, 39 different, each	7.5 x 80cm (3 x 31½in)
Fabric for bodies, 39 different, each	3.5 x 30cm (1⅜ x 12in)
Fabric for narrow border	6 x 520cm (2⅜ x 205in)
Fabric for broad border	11.5 x 580cm (4½ x 228½in)
Fabric for backing	145 x 200cm (57 x 78¾in)
Quilt wadding	135 x 190cm (53¼ x 74¾in)

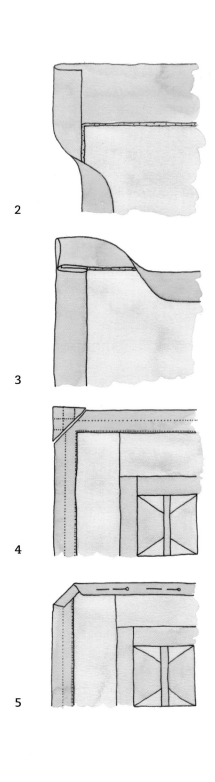

2

3

4

5

CLOSE APPLIQUÉ

This is an easy form of appliqué with a unique look. The technique is explained in full here, which you can use to make the three projects that follow: a placemat (page 92), a tea cosy (page 94) and an oven cloth (page 97). The materials list below is sufficient for the placemat.

The base for the appliqué could be a chequered patchwork of 16 squares as described overleaf or a single 21.5cm (8½in) square of fabric.

In this technique, flower shapes (petals) and separate flower centres and leaves are fused in place on the prepared base using fusible webbing such as Bondaweb. Once the design has been built up, with all the appliqué fabrics in place, you simply sew back and forth with lines of tight stitching. Choose a thread colour that matches the colour that you wish to accentuate. If, for example, red flowers are to remain red, sew with red thread. Other colours will appear slightly blurred. If you wish, sew a small sample or two first to help you decide on the colour choice.

The pattern for the flower, flower centre and leaf are provided on page 117.

MATERIALS

Chequered base

Fabric in colour A	6.5 x 55cm (2½ x 21½in)
Fabric in colour B	6.5 x 55cm (2½ x 21½in)
Volume fleece	22.5 x 22.5cm (9 x 9in)

Appliqué motif

Fabric for 6 flowers (petal shapes)	7.5 x 50cm (3 x 19¾in)
Fabric for 6 flower centres	4.5 x 25cm (1¾ x 10in)
Fabric for 6 leaves	6.5 x 26cm (2½ x 10¼in)
Fusible webbing (Vliesofix/Bondaweb)	20 x 52cm (8 x 20in)

MAKING THE CHEQUERED BASE

1 Sew the A and B fabric strips right sides together along one long edge.

2 Cut the piece in half to obtain two strips 27.5cm (10¾in) long. Pin the strips right sides together, with colour A against colour B, and sew together as shown in figure 1.

3 Press the seam allowances open.

4 From the joined piece, cut four strips, each 6.5cm (2½in) wide, as shown in figure 2. Discard the remnants.

5 Sew the strips right sides together as shown in figure 3 to create the chequered effect.

6 Press the seam allowances open. The joined base measures 21.5 x 21.5cm (8½ x 8½in).

7 Place the chequered piece wrong side down on the volume fleece and tack along the edges to secure the layers.

FUSING THE FLOWER MOTIFS

1 Iron the fusible webbing to the wrong side of the fabrics for the appliqué motifs.

2 Trace five or six flower shapes (petals) and the same number of flower centres on to the paper side of the fusible webbing, using the pattern on page 117. Trace four to six of the leaf shapes as well.

3 Cut out the shapes, peel the paper off and place the flowers, centres and leaves on the prepared base, making sure that the shapes do not extend to within 1.75cm (¾in) of the edges of the base fabric.

4 Iron all the parts in place (see figure 4).

STITCHING THE APPLIQUÉ

Set your sewing machine to a stitch length of 4 and work with 1–2mm (about ¹/₁₆in) between the lines of stitching.

1 Begin in the middle of the piece and sew back and forth in rows, stitching from one side to the other and working towards one end, as shown in figure 4.

2 Stitch over the other half of the design the same way.

3 Trim the piece, if necessary, so that the square format is preserved.

4 Stitch all round the square, 0.5cm (¼in) from the edge, using a stitch length of 1.5, to secure all the thread ends.

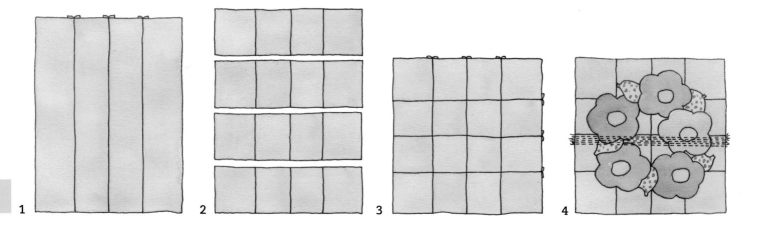

1   2   3   4

APPLIQUÉD PLACEMAT

Here we have a 28cm (11in) square placemat with space for a cup and a cake plate. First, you need to make a 21.5cm (8½in) floral appliqué, as described on pages 88–90, figures 1–4. Now you can add a border and backing to make the placemat following the instructions below.

ADDING THE BORDER

1 Iron the volume fleece for the border to the wrong side of the border fabric, so it follows one long edge (see figure 1). Divide the border fabric into four equally long pieces.
2 Place the first border strip right sides together with the appliquéd piece, so it extends one border width beyond the edge. Sew the border strip in place as shown in figure 2.

3 Press the border and the seam allowance outwards.
4 Attach the other three border strips right sides together with the appliquéd piece (see the detailed sequence on page 84, figures 2–5).
5 Fold the first border strip right sides together with the last one sewn on and complete the sewing of the first border strip (see figure 3).
6 Trim the piece so that it measures 30 x 30cm (12 x 12in).

ADDING THE BACKING

1 Iron the volume fleece for the backing to the wrong side of the backing fabric.
2 Use marker stitches to mark a 12cm (4¾in) wide opening on one edge of the front piece and backing.
3 Sew the appliquéd front and backing right sides together all round except between the marker stitching.
4 Trim off the corners diagonally (see figure 4).
5 Turn the placemat right side out and sew up the opening with slipstitches. Remove any visible marker stitches.
6 Topstitch around the appliquéd centre panel and around the outer edge of the placemat.

MATERIALS

For border and backing

Fabric for the border	6.5 x 105cm (2½ x 41½in)
Fabric for the backing	30 x 30cm (12 x 12in)
Volume fleece for the border	5.5 x 105cm (2¼ x 41½in)
Volume fleece for the backing	30 x 30cm (12 x 12in)

1

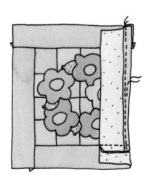

2

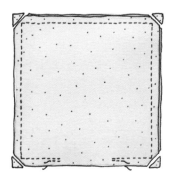

3

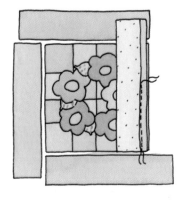

4

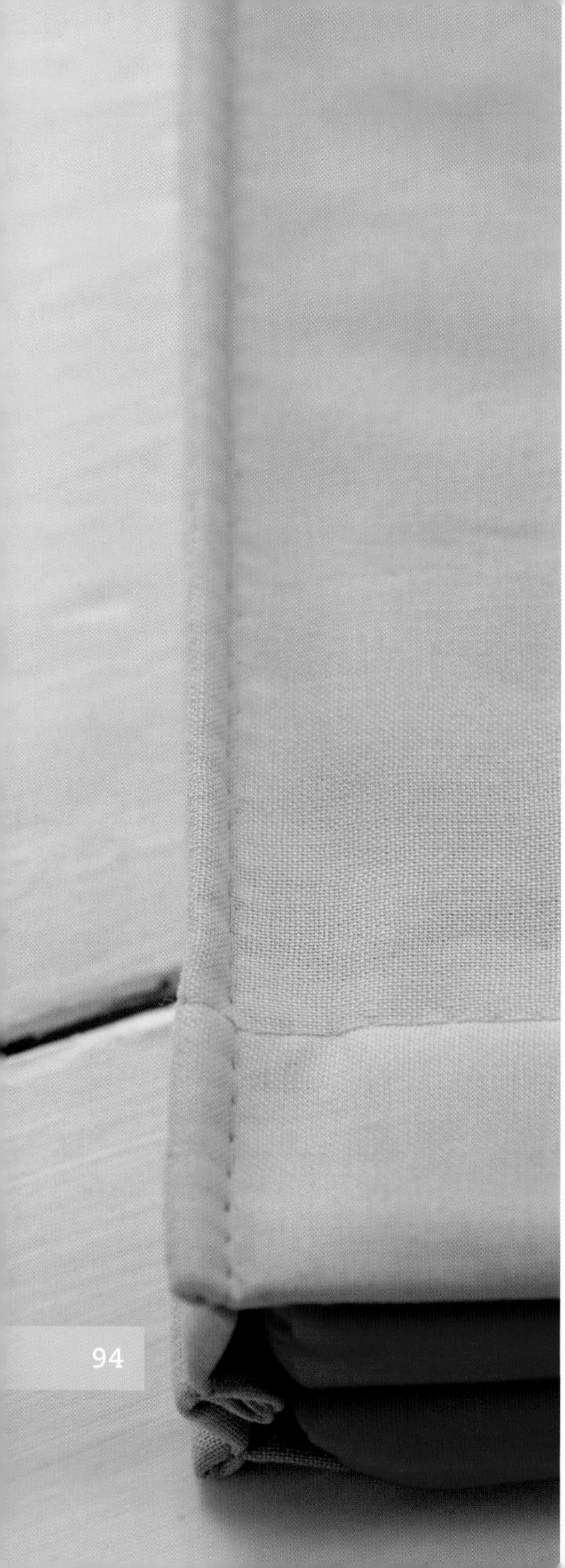

APPLIQUÉD TEA COSY

The tea cosy is 29cm (11½in) high, 33.5cm (13¼in) across and 3cm (1¼in) deep, and fits a 2-litre (3½-pint) teapot. The tea cosy consists of two parts: a lined cover and an inner insert that provides insulation.

The cover has an appliquéd centre panel, which features 24 flowers, and side panels with pin tucks. The flowers are prepared as described on page 90. For this model, seven different colours are used for the flower petals and three different colours for the flower centres.

The insulated insert is made from dense foam. This can be bought from an upholsterer who will cut it to the desired size.

The pattern for the flowers (petals) and flower centres are provided on page 117.

MATERIALS

Fabric for the centre panel	24 x 68cm (9½ x 26¾in)
Fabric for lining the centre panel	24 x 68cm (9½ x 26¾in)
Fabric for the flowers	8.5 x 180cm (3½ x 71in)
Fabric for the flower centres	3.5 x 100cm (1½ x 39½in)
Fabric for outer side panels, 2 pieces	11 x 66cm (4¼ x 26in)
Fabric for lining the side panels, 2 pieces	11 x 66cm (4¼ x 26in)
Fabric for binding, 2 pieces	3 x 40cm (1¼ x 16in)
Fusible webbing (Vliesofix/Bondaweb)	12 x 180cm (4¾ x 71in)
Volume fleece for the centre panel	24 x 68cm (9½ x 26¾in)
Volume fleece for the side panel, 2 pieces	9 x 66cm (3½ x 26in)

Insulated insert

Foam sheet, 1cm (⅜in) thick	32.5 x 58cm (12¾ x 22¾in)
Fabric for the insert cover	35 x 119.5cm (13¾ x 47in)

MAKING THE CENTRE PANEL

1 Iron the volume fleece for the centre panel on to the wrong side of the centre panel fabric.

2 Place the wrong side of the lining against the other side of the volume fleece and tack the layers together.

3 Prepare 24 flowers and flower centres from your chosen fabrics (see page 90).

4 Lay out the flowers and flower centres, keeping 4cm (1½in) free at the short ends of the panel. Flowers can be trimmed and placed at the sides, as shown in figure 1.

5 Appliqué the flowers in place as described on page 90.

6 Trim the panel to measure 22 x 66cm (8½ x 26in).

7 Sew all around the panel, 0.5cm (¼in) from the edge, with a stitch length of 1.5 to secure all the threads.

ATTACHING THE SIDE PANELS

1 Iron the volume fleece for the side panels to the wrong side of each of the two side panels as shown on the left of figure 2.

2 Place the panels right sides together with the centre panel and pin them in place.

3 Place the lining panels right sides together with the lining side of the centre panel.

4 Sew the centre panel to the side panels.

5 Fold the panels out and topstitch on each side of the centre panel as shown on the right of figure 2.

ATTACHING THE BINDING

1 Sew a binding strip to one short end of the tea cosy with right sides facing (see figure 3).

2 Fold the binding over to the back and tack in place.

3 Fold a 2.5cm (1in) hem to the wrong side of the tea cosy along the same edge (see figure 4).

4 Sew the hem in place and remove any visible tacking thread.

5 Attach the second binding strip to the other end of the tea cosy in the same way.

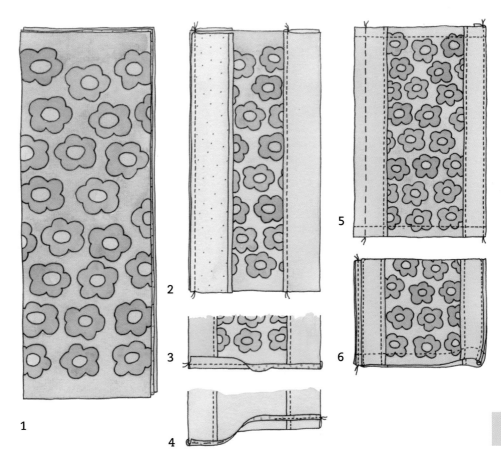

1

2

3

4

5

6

COMPLETING THE TEA COSY COVER

1 Measure 6.5cm (2½in) out from the centre panel and sew marker stitching along the length of the side panel as shown on the left of figure 5, page 95.
2 Repeat on the other side panel.
3 Fold one side panel towards the back, so the marker stitching is lying just on top of the fold. Machine stitch 0.5cm (¼in) from the fold as shown on the right in figure 5, page 95, to make a pin tuck.
4 Repeat on the other panel and remove the marker stitching.
5 Fold the piece lining sides together and sew the side seams, taking a 0.5cm (¼in) seam allowance as shown on the left of figure 6, page 95.

6 Trim the raw edges close to the seam stitching and turn the tea cosy lining side up.
7 Sew the side seams again, using a presser foot's seam allowance, as shown on the right in figure 6. This completes the French seams.
8 Turn the tea cosy right side out.

MAKING THE INSERT

This simple insert is a thin sheet of foam with a fabric cover. It shapes and insulates the tea cosy.

1 Sew marker stitching along the short ends of the insert fabric, 0.5cm (¼in) from the edge.

2 Press a seam allowance to the wrong side, so the marker stitching is lying just on top of the fold.
3 Fold the fabric right sides together, as shown in figure 7, and sew both long side seams.
4 Press the seam allowances open and turn right side out.
5 Fit the foam sheet inside the cover.
6 Sew up the opening with slipstitches.
7 Stuff the corners of the cover in and sew in place with slipstitches.
8 Fold the insulation insert in the middle, as shown in figure 8, and insert it into the lined tea cosy.

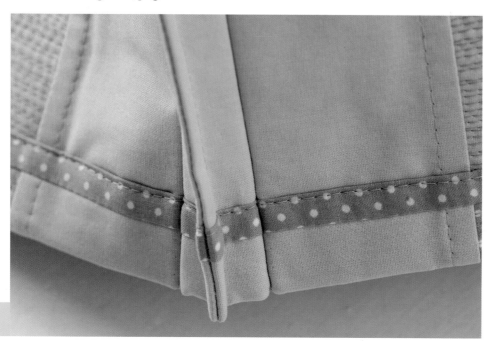

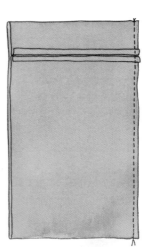

7

8

APPLIQUÉD OVEN CLOTH

This insulated cloth is designed for holding the teapot's hot handle and has appliquéd flowers and leaves as described on page 90. It is 17cm (6¾in) square.

MATERIALS

Fabric for the front	20 x 20cm (8 x 8in)
Fabric for the flowers (petals)	7.5 x 45cm (3 x 17¾in)
Fabric for the flower centres	4.5 x 20cm (1¾ x 8in)
Fabric for the leaves	6.5 x 26cm (2½ x 10¼in)
Fabric for the backing	19 x 19cm (7½ x 7½in)
Insulated wadding	22 x 22cm (8¾ x 8¾in)
Fusible webbing (Vliesofix/Bondaweb)	20 x 46cm (8 x 18in)
Volume fleece	19 x 19cm (7½ x 7½in)

MAKING THE OVEN CLOTH

1 Tack the front fabric centrally on to the insulated wadding.

2 Prepare and appliqué five flowers and flower centres, as well as five or six leaves, following the instructions on page 90.

3 Trim the front piece to measure 19 x 19cm (7½ x 7½in).

4 Stitch all round the piece 0.5cm (¼in) from the edge, using a stitch length of 1.5, to secure the threads.

5 Iron the volume fleece to the wrong side of the backing fabric.

6 Work marker stitching on the front and back to mark a 10cm (4in) wide opening (see the illustration below).

7 Sew the front and back right sides together, except where the marker stitches show the opening.

8 Trim the corners off diagonally in the seam allowances and turn right side out.

9 Close up the opening with slipstitches.

10 Topstitch all round, a presser foot's seam allowance from the edges to finish.

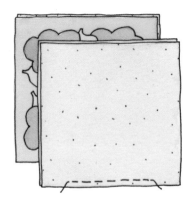

STARS

This delightful design enables you to use up those tiny pieces of leftover fabric that were too nice to throw away. The remnants are used as they are, so some tips are small and others large, the result being that each star is unique.

Materials are provided for three sizes that can be combined in many ways. The small star panel is 13.5 x 13.5cm (5¼ x 5¼in), the medium-sized panel is 25 x 25cm (10 x 10in) and the large panel is 37 x 37cm (14½ x 14½in).

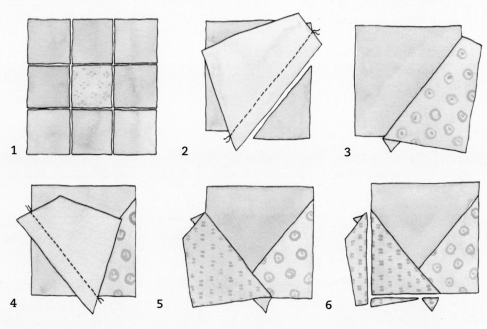

MATERIALS

Per star panel	Small	Medium	Large
Fabric for the base colour	5.5 x 44cm (2¼ x 18in)	9.5 x 76cm (3¾ x 30in)	13.5 x 108cm (5¼ x 42in)
Fabric for the centre square	5.5 x 5.5cm (2¼ x 2¼in)	9.5 x 9.5cm (3¾ x 3¾in)	13.5 x 13.5cm (5¼ x 5¼in)
Small fabric remnants			

MAKING THE STAR PANEL

1 Divide the base fabric into eight squares, 5.5cm (2¼in), 9.5cm (3¾in) or 13.5cm (5¼in), depending on the size you are making.

2 Lay out the squares and the centre panel as shown in figure 1.

3 Find a fabric remnant and place it right sides together with a square in the base colour as shown in figure 2. Test fold and make sure that the fabric remnant (the point of the star) reaches far enough out to cover the corner of the square.

4 Sew the seam and then trim the square to the seam allowance (see figure 2).

5 Press the seam allowance open so the point of the star is folded out (see figure 3).

6 Trim the point of the star to size so the square shape is maintained.

7 Place a new fabric remnant on and sew in place as shown in figure 4.

8 Trim the square to the seam allowance.

9 Press the seam allowance open and trim the point of the star to size so the square shape is maintained (see figures 5 and 6).

10 Sew points on to a further three squares in the base colour in the same way.

11 Join the squares together in rows (see figure 7).

12 Press the seam allowances open.

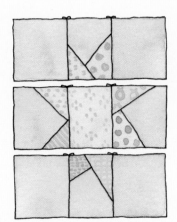

7

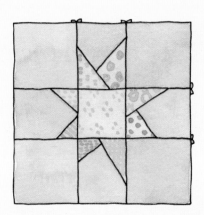

8

STAR TABLE RUNNER

This super table runner combines star panels of all three sizes: eight small, one medium and two large stars.

MAKING THE STAR PATCHWORK

1 Cut the fabric in the base colour into strips of the size required for each star: eight strips 5.5cm (2¼in) wide for the small stars plus two strips 13.5cm (5¼in) wide for the large stars – the strip for the medium star is already the right width.

2 Cut all the base-colour strips into squares.

3 Sew eight small, one medium and two large star panels following the instructions on pages 98–99, figures 1–8.

4 Arrange the stars as shown in the illustration on the left and stitch them together. This arrangement measures approximately 37.5 x 121.5cm (14¾ x 48in).

ASSEMBLING THE TABLE RUNNER

1 Iron the volume fleece to the back of the star patchwork.

2 Measure a 12cm (4¾in) opening on the star patchwork and on the backing fabric along one edge.

3 Sew marker stitches to mark the opening.

4 Place the star patchwork right sides together with the backing fabric and sew together, except across the opening.

5 Trim the corners off diagonally in the seam allowances and turn right side out.

6 Slipstitch the opening closed.

7 Quilt around the stars and around the edge.

MATERIALS

Stars	8 small	1 medium	2 large
Fabric in the base colour	44 x 44cm	9.5 x 76cm	27 x 108cm
	(18 x 18in)	(3¾ x 30in)	(10½ x 42in)
Fabric for the centre panels	5.5 x 44cm	9.5 x 9.5cm	13.5 x 27cm
	(2¼ x 17½in)	(3¾ x 3¾in)	(5¼ x 10½in)
Small fabric remnants			

Additional materials

Volume fleece	37.5 x 121.5cm (14¾ x 48in)
Fabric for the backing	37.5 x 121.5cm (14¾ x 48in)

COFFEE COSY WITH STARS

This coffee cosy is 29cm (11½in) high, 25cm (10in) across and 3cm (1¼in) deep, and fits a 1-litre (1¾ pint) cafetière. It is similar to the tea cosy on pages 94–96 and consists of a cover over an insulated insert. The patchwork on the coffee cosy features a centre panel with four small stars and bars. Make the star panels as described on pages 98–99, figures 1–8. Side panels are sewn on to each side of the centre panel.

MAKING THE STAR PATCHWORK

1 Sew the star panels together in pairs to make two pairs of stars.
2 From the fabric for the dividing bars, cut a strip 5 x 13.5cm (2 x 5¼in).
3 Place the strip right sides together with one of the pairs of stars and sew together.
4 Sew the other pair of stars to the other side of the dividing bar. Press the seam allowances of both seams just sewn towards the dividing bar.
5 Cut two end bars each 8.5 x 13.5cm (3¼ x 5¼in) from the remaining fabric for the bars.
6 Place one end bar right sides together with a pair of stars and sew together. Sew the second bar on to the end of the other pair of stars (see the illustration opposite).

ADDING THE LINING AND SIDE PANELS

1 Iron the lining and volume fleece together.
2 Centre the piece with the star patchwork (centre panel) on the lining, on the side with the volume fleece.
3 Quilt and topstitch around the stars and bars as shown in the photograph.
4 Place a side panel right sides together with the star piece and sew together.
5 Press the piece out and topstitch.
6 Attach the other side panel in the same way.
7 Trim the piece to the dimensions 32.5 x 66cm (12¾ x 26in).

BINDING THE ENDS

Attach the binding strips to the short ends of the patchwork as described on page 95, figures 3 and 4.

COMPLETING THE COFFEE COSY COVER

1 Measure 3cm (1¼in) in from each long edge of the patchwork and mark a line with a marking needle.
2 Sew marker stitching at the marks (see the illustration opposite).
3 Fold one side so the marker stitching is just on top of the fold (see figure 5 on page 95).
4 Sew a pin tuck 0.5cm (¼in) deep.
5 Sew a pin tuck along the other side in the same way.
6 Remove the marker stitching.
7 Fold the piece lining sides together and sew the side seams, taking a

MATERIALS

4 small star panels, each	13.5 x 13.5cm (5¼ x 5¼in)
Fabric for the bars	13.5 x 25cm (5¼ x 10in)
Fabric for the lining	33 x 67cm (13 x 26½in)
Volume fleece	33 x 67cm (13 x 26½in)
Fabric for the side panels, 2 pieces	12 x 66cm (4¾ x 26in)
Fabric for the binding, 2 pieces	3 x 32cm (1¼ x 12½in)

Insulated insert

Foam sheet, 1cm (³/₈in) thick	24 x 58cm (9½ x 22¾in)
Fabric for the insert cover	26.5 x 119.5cm (10¼ x 47in)

0.5cm (¼in) seam allowance as shown on the left of figure 6 on page 95.

8 Trim the raw edges close to the seam.

9 Now fold the cover right sides together and sew the side seams again, taking a presser foot's seam allowance as shown on the right in figure 6 on page 95. This completes the French seams.

10 Turn the coffee cosy right side out.

MAKING THE INSERT

This is simply a foam sheet with a fabric cover that is folded and pushed into the coffee cosy. It shapes and insulates the cosy. Follow the instructions on page 96, figures 7 and 8.

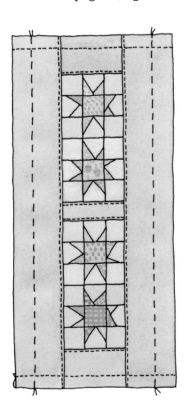

ROSETTES

These rosettes may look different, but all of them have 16 leaves or petals. The variations occur by changing the length of the leaf pattern.

The instructions are for three variations. The first two rosettes are the same except that the first one has a small centre with long leaves and the second has a large centre with short leaves. The third variation is a multicoloured rosette with a medium-sized centre.

These rosettes can be appliquéd on to the front of a cushion (see pages 108–109), or an extra-large rosette can be appliquéd on to a pouffe (pages 110–113). As a further refinement, the rosettes can be appliquéd on to a segmented base (see page 108).

The pattern for the rosette leaf, which includes seam allowances, is on page 116.

MATERIALS

Centre size	Small	Medium	Large
Fabric for leaves, 16 different	10.5 x 17cm (4¼ x 6¾in)		
Fabric for leaves			9 x 135cm (3½ x 53¼in)
Fabric for the inner leaves, 4 the same		5.5 x 42cm (2¼ x 16½in)	
Fabric for the outer leaves, 4 different		11 x 42cm (4¼ x 16½in)	
Rosette centre			
Cardboard for a template	8 x 8cm (3¼ x 3¼in)	12 x 12cm (4¾ x 4¾in)	24 x 24cm (9½ x 9½in)
Volume fleece	8 x 8cm (3¼ x 3¼in)	12 x 12cm (4¾ x 4¾in)	24 x 24cm (9½ x 9½in)
Fabric for the centre	9 x 9cm (3½ x 3½in)	13 x 13cm (5⅛in x 5⅛in)	26 x 26cm (10¼ x 10¼in)

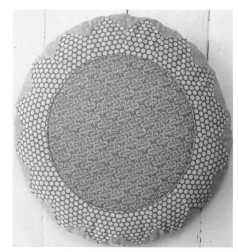

MAKING A ROSETTE WITH A SMALL OR LARGE CENTRE

The rosette leaves for these two options are cut to different lengths but sewn in the same way.

1 Using the pattern on page 116, cut 16 rosette leaves with small or large centres, depending on your chosen variation (see figures 1 and 2).
2 Fold a leaf lengthways, right sides together and sew as shown in figure 3.
3 Press the seam allowance open (see figure 4) and turn right side out.
4 Sew another 15 leaves in the same way.

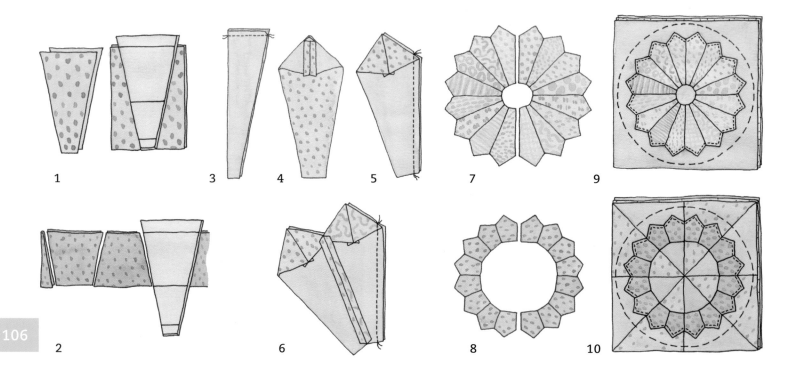

1

2

3

4

5

6

7

8

9

10

5 Sew the leaves together in pairs with right sides facing (see figure 5).
6 Press the seam allowances open as you go and sew all the pairs right sides together into quarter rosettes (see figure 6).
7 Sew the quarter rosettes together in pairs to make two half rosettes. Figure 7 shows a small centre and figure 8 a large centre.
8 Sew the half rosettes together to complete the ring.
9 Save the rosette for later appliqué.

MAKING THE MULTICOLOURED ROSETTE

The inner leaves or petals on this rosette are made from one fabric while the outer ones are cut from four different but coordinating fabrics. Use the pattern for the rosette leaf with a medium-sized centre.

1 Place each strip for the outer leaves right sides together with a strip for the inner leaves, matching the long edges.

2 Sew the two pieces together and press the seam allowances open.
3 Using the medium-sized pattern from page 116, cut four rosette leaves from each of the joined strips, as shown in figure 11.
4 Shape and join the leaves, following the instructions for the other rosettes, and as shown in figures 3–6 and 12.
5 Sew the half rosettes together to complete the ring.
6 Save the rosette for later appliqué.

ADDING THE FLOWER CENTRE

1 Cut out a circle of cardboard to the diameter required – 7cm (2¾in) for the rosette with a small centre, 23.5cm (9¼in) for the large centre or 11cm (4⅜in) for the medium centre.
2 Cut out a circle in the volume fleece using the cardboard template. Centre it on the wrong side of the fabric for the flower centre and iron it in place.
3 Cut out the fabric around the fleece, adding a seam allowance all round.
4 Tack and press the flower centre as described on page 11, figures 9a–9c.
5 Set the centre aside for later appliqué.

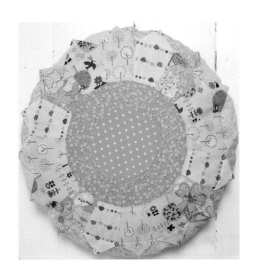

11

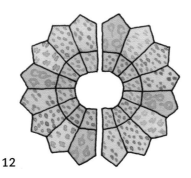

12

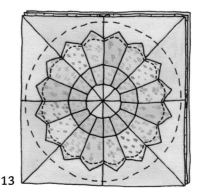

13

ROSETTE CUSHIONS

The rosettes from the previous project look splendid appliquéd on to this simple round cushion. First, the rosette of your choice needs to be appliquéd on to the front cushion piece and then you can add the back, which has a simple button opening to make laundering easier. The cushion front can either be cut from a single piece of fabric or segmented like cake slices (see below). The cushion cover fits a 40cm (16in) round cushion pad.

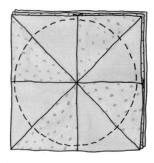

1

2

MATERIALS

Front

	Segmented	Plain
Fabric in colour A, 2 pieces	23.5 x 23.5cm (9¼ x 9¼in)	
Fabric in colour B, 2 pieces	23.5 x 23.5cm (9¼ x 9¼in)	
Fabric for a plain base		43 x 43cm (17 x 17in)
Volume fleece	43 x 43cm (17 x 17in)	43 x 43cm (17 x 17in)
Fabric for lining	43 x 43cm (17 x 17in)	43 x 43cm (17 x 17in)

Back cover

Main fabric, 2 pieces	24 x 43cm (9½ x 17in)
Fabric for lining, 2 pieces	24 x 43cm (9½ x 17in)
3 buttons, press studs or Velcro tapes	2.5 x 31cm (1 x 12¼in)
Cushion pad diameter	40cm (16in)

MAKING A SEGMENTED BASE
1 Join each square in one fabric to a square of the other fabric diagonally, and then cut and press the seams open to make half square triangle units as explained on page 11, figures 10a–10d.
2 Stitch the new squares together in pairs and sew the pairs together as shown in figure 1.

PREPARING THE FRONT BASE
1 Draw a circle on the base fabric (segmented or plain) with a diameter of 42cm (16½in).
2 Iron the volume fleece to the wrong side of the base fabric and place the lining underneath the volume fleece.
3 Sew marker stitching along the line that marks the circle (see figures 1 and 2).

ATTACHING THE ROSETTE
1 Centre a prepared rosette on the base as shown in figures 9 and 10 on page 106 and in figure 13 on page 107.
2 Appliqué the rosette of leaves in place by stitching around the outer edge.
3 Centre a prepared flower centre on the rosette and appliqué it in place.

MAKING AND ATTACHING THE BACK
The back is made from two identical pieces that overlap in the centre of the back by 3cm (1¼in) to form the opening.

The cover can be closed with Velcro tapes, press studs or buttons. Make the back pieces first and then join them to the front as explained here.

1 Stitch each back piece right sides together with a back lining along one long edge (see the top illustration in figure 3).
2 Press the seam allowances open, turn right side out and tack along the joined edge as shown in the second illustration in figure 3.
3 Mark a 30cm (12in) wide opening in the middle of the joined edge on both pieces.
4 Sew three buttons and corresponding buttonholes or press studs on each piece, 1.5cm (⅝in) from the edge, as shown in figure 4. Alternatively, stitch Velcro tapes in place with two lines of stitching (see figure 5).
5 Join the two back pieces by closing the fastenings and sew on both sides of the opening as shown on the right in figure 5.
6 Pin the front cushion piece and the back cover lining sides together.
7 Sew together all round, following the marker stitches on the front.
8 Trim the seam allowance back to 3mm (⅛in).
9 Turn the cover lining side out and sew the outside seam again, taking a 0.5cm (¼in) seam allowance.
10 Turn the cover right side out and slip the cushion pad inside.

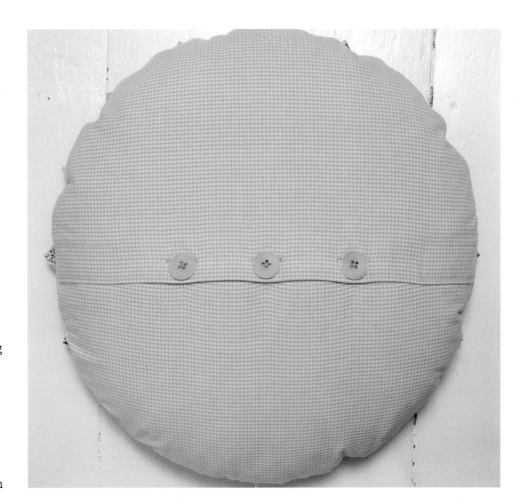

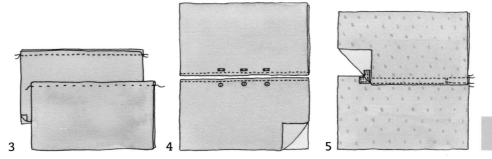

3   4   5

ROSETTE POUFFE

This pouffe is cleverly made so that the cover can be easily removed for cleaning. The inner pouffe is made from heavy denim for strength and durability and is stuffed very firmly. The removable cover is made in a sturdy upholstery fabric in two parts, joined with Velcro tapes. The pouffe is 45cm (17¾in) in diameter and 26cm (10¼in) high.

MAKING THE POUFFE

First, you need to make the stuffed pouffe foundation from the denim fabric, then make the patchwork rosette appliqué and apply it to the fabric for the top of the cover, and finally make and assemble the cover. The rosette can be stabilised with interfacing, which should be ironed on to the wrong side of the fabric before the leaves are cut. The pattern for the rosette leaf includes seam allowances and can be found on page 116.

MATERIALS

Foundation pouffe

Fabric (denim or similar)	100 x 110cm (39½ x 43¼in)
Fibrefill	2.5–3kg (4½ –6½lb)

Removable cover

Fabric for the rosette, colour A	17 x 70cm (6¾ x 27½in)
Fabric for the rosette, colour B	17 x 70cm (6¾ x 27½in)
Fabric for the centre, colour C	9 x 18cm (3½ x 7in)
Fabric for the centre, colour D	9 x 18cm (3½ x 7in)
Interfacing for the rosette	17 x 140cm (6¾ x 55in)
Cardboard	13 x 13cm (5 x 5in)
Volume fleece	13 x 13cm (5 x 5in)
Fabric for the cover	100 x 130cm (39½ x 51¾in)
Velcro tapes	150cm (59in)

MAKING THE FOUNDATION POUFFE

1 Divide the fabric into two pieces, each measuring 50 x 50cm (19¾ x 19¾in), and two pieces each measuring 27 x 75cm (10¾ x 29½in), as shown in figure 1.

2 Draw and cut out two circles with a diameter of 47cm (18½in) from the square pieces of fabric.

3 Sew the 27 x 75cm (10¾ x 29½in) rectangles together with right sides facing along the short edges to make a ring, leaving an 18cm (7in) opening in one seam (see figure 2).

4 Press the seam allowances open and topstitch them in place.

5 Divide the ring and one of the circles into four equal sections and mark with pins (see figure 3).

6 Match the circle to the ring with right sides together at the marker pins as shown in figure 3. Insert more pins and sew together.

7 Press the seam allowances on to the circle and topstitch them in place.

8 Mark, sew and topstitch the ring together with the other circle in the same way.

9 Turn the pouffe right side out.

10 Stuff the pouffe very firmly with fibrefill, forming it into a cylindrical shape with a flat top and bottom (see figure 4).

11 Close the opening with slipstitch.

MAKING THE ROSETTE

1 Iron the interfacing to the wrong side of the fabric.

2 Cut eight rosette leaves in colour A and eight in colour B using the pattern on page 116 (see figure 5).

3 Sew the leaves together as described on pages 106–107, figures 3–6, and as shown here in figure 6.

4 Join the half rosettes together to complete the ring of leaves.

MAKING THE SEGMENTED FLOWER CENTRE

1 Divide the fabric for the centre, colours C and D, into 9 x 9cm (3½ x 3½in) squares.

2 Pair up the squares with right sides facing, using one fabric in each colour. Stitch the squares diagonally and cut and press the seams open to make half square triangle units as described on page 11, figures 10a–10d.

3 Sew the squares together into a segmented piece, like cake slices (see figure 7).

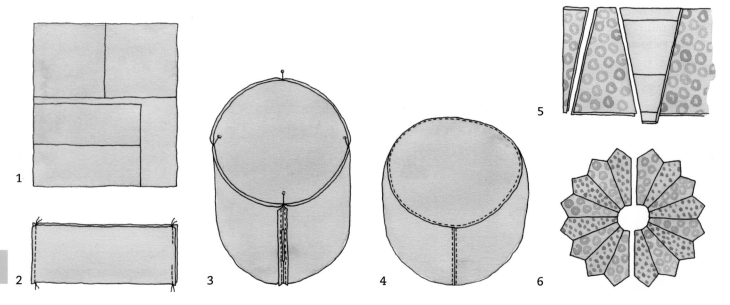

1 2 3 4 5 6

4 Cut a circle out of the cardboard and volume fleece with a diameter of 12cm (4¾in).

5 Centre the volume fleece on the wrong side of the segmented square and iron it in place.

6 Cut out the fabric circle, adding a seam allowance all round.

7 Tack and press a centre as described on page 11, figures 9a–9c.

8 Set the rosette and flower centre aside for later appliqué.

ASSEMBLING THE COVER

1 Divide the fabric for the cover into two pieces each 50 x 50cm (19¾ x 19¾in), two pieces each 30 x 75cm (12 x 29½in) and two pieces each 10 x 75cm (4 x 29½in) as shown in figure 8.

2 Draw and cut out two circles with a diameter of 47cm (18½in) from the square pieces of fabric.

3 Zigzag around the edges of all the fabric pieces to prevent fraying.

4 Centre and appliqué the rosette and then the flower centre on to one of the circles as shown in figure 9.

5 Sew the 30 x 75cm (12 x 29½in) rectangles into a ring by joining the short edges with right sides together.

6 Press the seam allowances open and topstitch them in place.

7 Divide the ring and the circle into four equal sections and mark with pins (see figure 3).

8 Match the circle to the ring with right sides together at the marker pins. Insert more pins and sew together.

9 Press the seam allowance on to the circle and topstitch it in place.

10 Fold and tack 2.5cm (1in) to the wrong side at the bottom of the cover.

11 Split the Velcro tapes apart and position the soft part to cover the raw edge of the fabric fold. Put pins in as far as is possible (see figure 10).

12 Sew the Velcro tape in place along the sides. As you go, adjust the length to about 148cm (58¼in).

13 Sew the 10 x 75cm (4 x 29½in) fabric strips together into a ring, right sides together.

14 Press the seam allowances open and topstitch them in place.

15 Divide the last circle and the ring in four equal parts as before and mark with pins.

16 Match the circle and the ring right sides together at the pins. Insert more pins and sew together.

17 Press the seam allowance on to the circle and topstitch it in place.

18 Position the Velcro tape 1.5cm (⅝in) up on the side and put pins in as far as is possible (see figure 11).

19 Sew the Velcro tape in place along the sides. As you go, adjust the length to about 148cm (58¼in).

20 Turn both pieces of the pouffe right side out.

21 Slip the cover on to the foundation cushion and fasten the Velcro tapes together to finish.

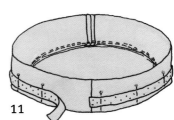
10

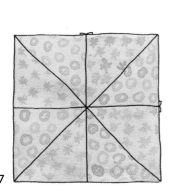
7

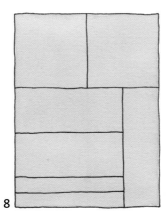
8

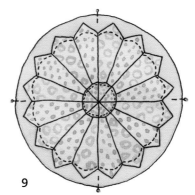
9

11

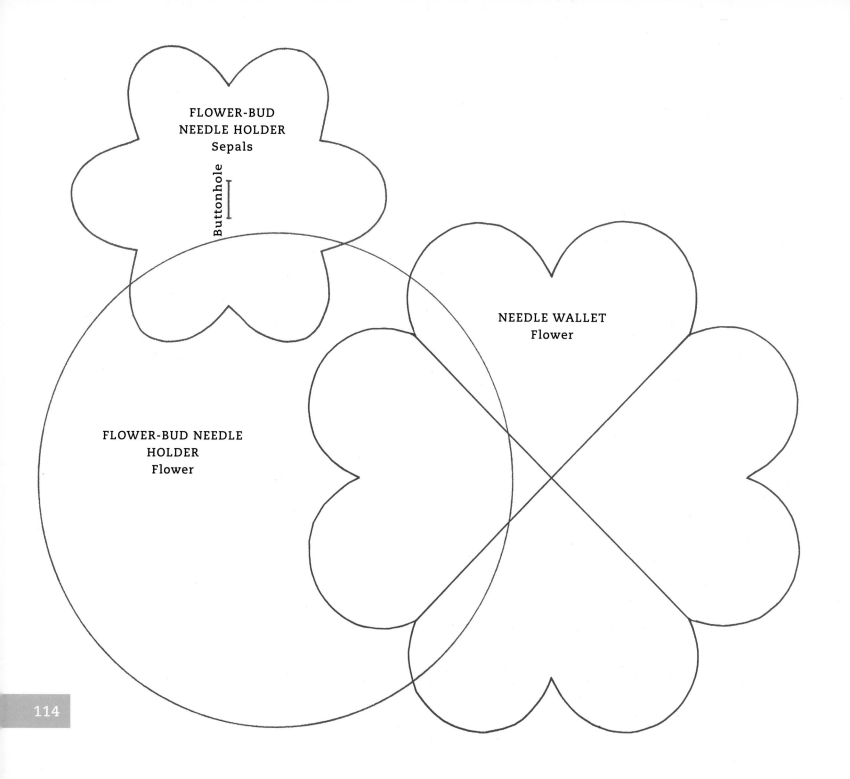

FLOWER-BUD
NEEDLE HOLDER
Sepals

Buttonhole

NEEDLE WALLET
Flower

FLOWER-BUD NEEDLE
HOLDER
Flower

114

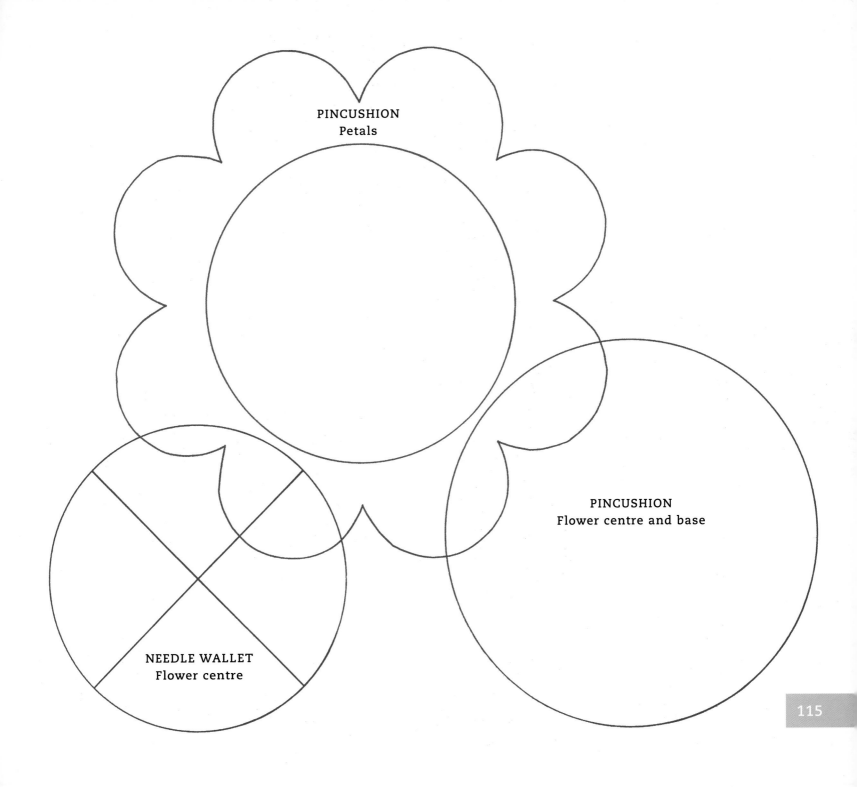

PINCUSHION
Petals

PINCUSHION
Flower centre and base

NEEDLE WALLET
Flower centre

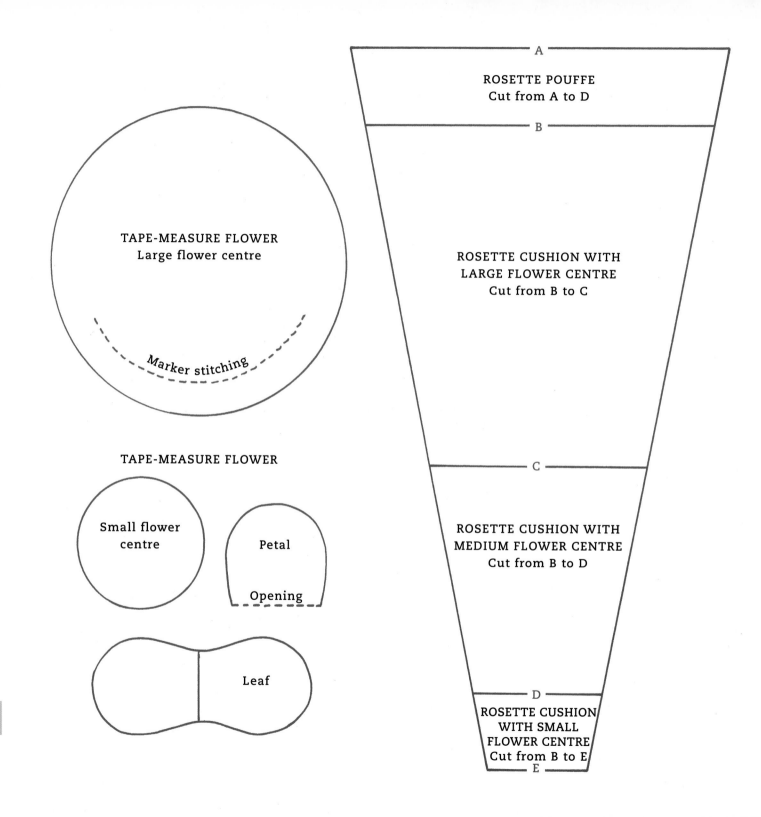

TAPE-MEASURE FLOWER
Large flower centre

Marker stitching

TAPE-MEASURE FLOWER

Small flower centre

Petal

Opening

Leaf

ROSETTE POUFFE
Cut from A to D

ROSETTE CUSHION WITH
LARGE FLOWER CENTRE
Cut from B to C

ROSETTE CUSHION WITH
MEDIUM FLOWER CENTRE
Cut from B to D

ROSETTE CUSHION
WITH SMALL
FLOWER CENTRE
Cut from B to E

A

B

C

D

E

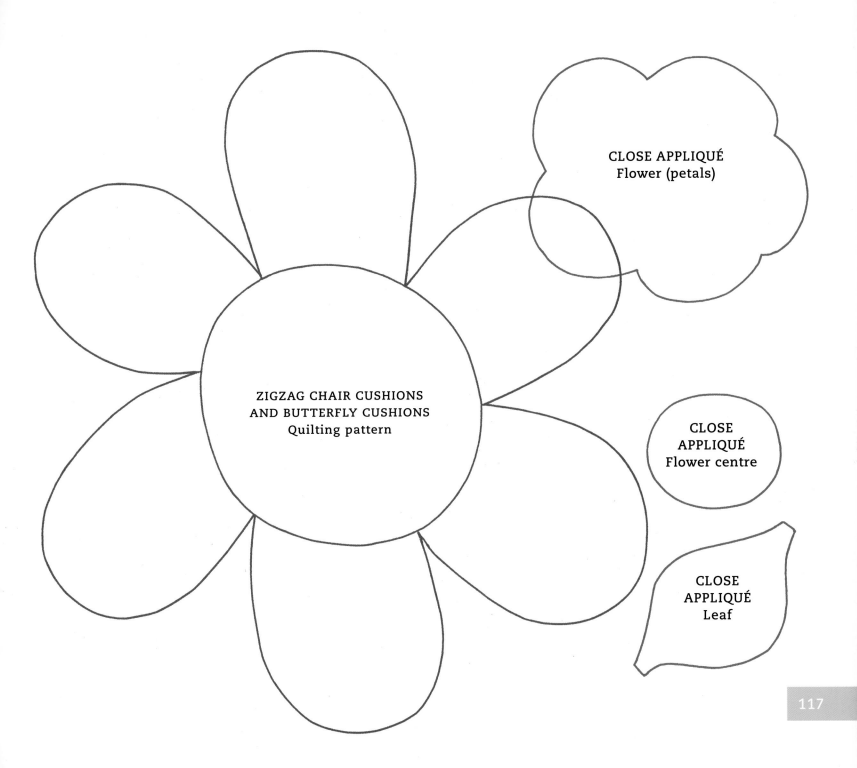

CLOSE APPLIQUÉ
Flower (petals)

ZIGZAG CHAIR CUSHIONS
AND BUTTERFLY CUSHIONS
Quilting pattern

CLOSE
APPLIQUÉ
Flower centre

CLOSE
APPLIQUÉ
Leaf

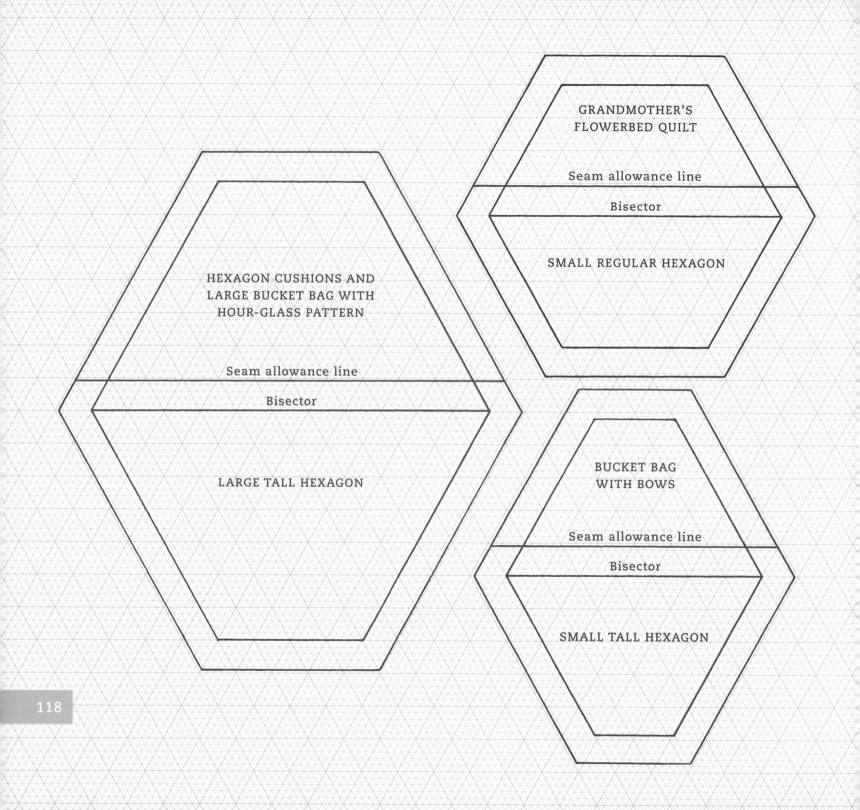

GRANDMOTHER'S
FLOWERBED QUILT

Seam allowance line

Bisector

SMALL REGULAR HEXAGON

HEXAGON CUSHIONS AND
LARGE BUCKET BAG WITH
HOUR-GLASS PATTERN

Seam allowance line

Bisector

LARGE TALL HEXAGON

BUCKET BAG
WITH BOWS

Seam allowance line

Bisector

SMALL TALL HEXAGON

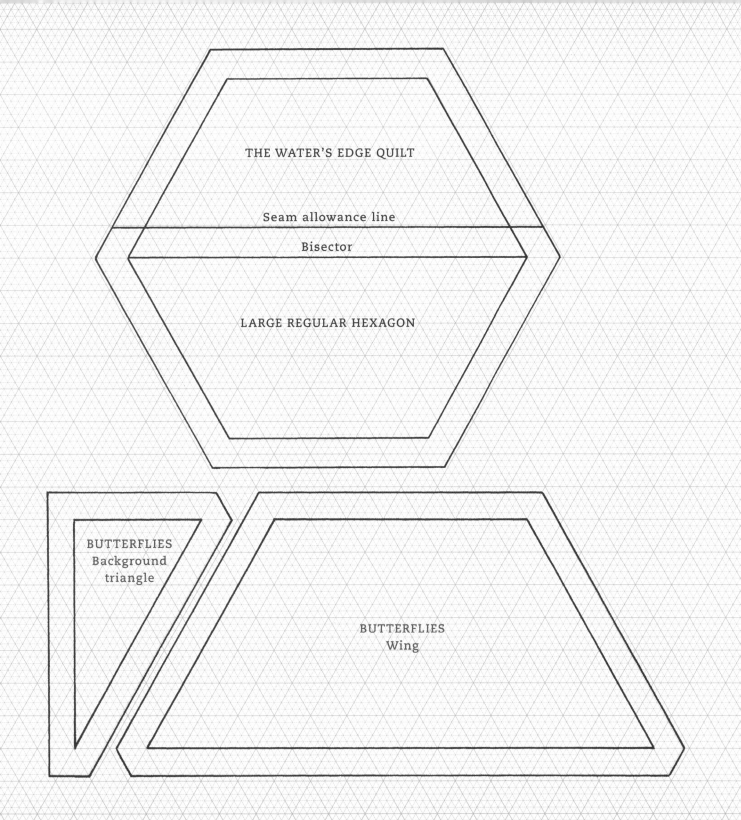

THE WATER'S EDGE QUILT

Seam allowance line

Bisector

LARGE REGULAR HEXAGON

BUTTERFLIES
Background
triangle

BUTTERFLIES
Wing

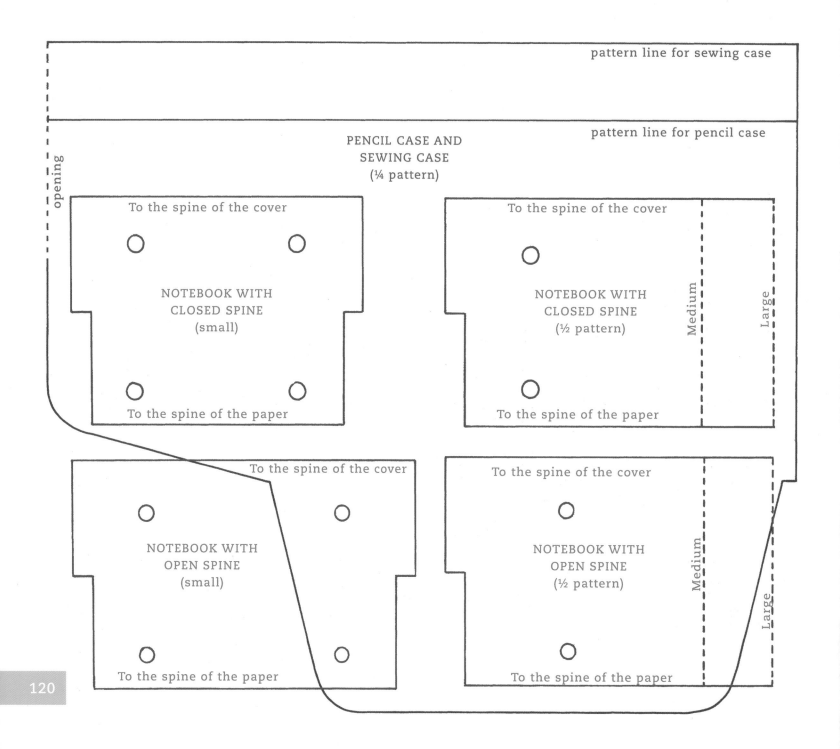

pattern line for sewing case

pattern line for pencil case

PENCIL CASE AND
SEWING CASE
(¼ pattern)

opening

To the spine of the cover

NOTEBOOK WITH
CLOSED SPINE
(small)

To the spine of the paper

To the spine of the cover

NOTEBOOK WITH
CLOSED SPINE
(½ pattern)

Medium

Large

To the spine of the paper

To the spine of the cover

NOTEBOOK WITH
OPEN SPINE
(small)

To the spine of the paper

To the spine of the cover

NOTEBOOK WITH
OPEN SPINE
(½ pattern)

Medium

Large

To the spine of the paper